3 1336 00171 8155

D0535130

THE COUNCIL AND THE MASS

By the same Author

Holy Week: A Commentary. Browne & Nolan, 1959

THE COUNCIL

AND

THE MASS

by

DOM MARK TIERNEY, O.S.B.

DIMENSION BOOKS INC.
WILKES-BARRE, PA. 1965

First American Edition 1965

Library of Congress Catalog Number 65-2556 I

IMPRIMI POTEST

✠JOSEPH DOWDALL, O.S.B. ABBAS ABBATIAE S. COLUMBAE GLENSTAL, DIE 6 JANUARII, 1965. NIHIL OBSTAT JACOBUS RYAN, D.D. CENSOR DEPUTATUS. IMPRIMATUR ✠THOMAS MORRIS ARCHIEPISCOPUS CASSILIENSIS ET IMOLACENSIS. THURLESIAE, DIE 8 JANUARII, 1965

TABLE OF CONTENTS

APPENDICES

INTRODUCTION

This little book is an attempt to apply the principles of the Constitution on the Sacred Liturgy of Vatican II to the Mass. It also takes into consideration the Instruction for the Proper Implementing of the Liturgy Constitution and the directives of the bishops.

All the commentaries which have appeared so far have dealt with the Constitution as a whole. I have limited myself to those parts of the Constitution which bear upon the Mass alone. I have, however, been able to draw on the information contained in the *Ephermerides Liturgicae, La Maison-Dieu, Worship, Doctrine and Life* and on Father Crichton's *The Church's Worship,* in so far as they relate to the Mass. The bibliography at the end of the book will indicate how indebted I am to others for many points of detail.

The Constitution is not so much the end of the road as the beginning, the point of departure. It opens up a new era in liturgical studies, thought and action. The Church has not turned her back upon the past, rather has she sought to restore what was best in her traditions to suit modern needs. What she proposes is both old and new, old wine in new bottles.

This book is not intended as a commentary on the Constitution, but rather as an effort to see its pastoral implications for the Catholic Church in America today. Time alone will prove how successful the reforms will be. We must admit, however, there are human as well as divine elements at work in restoring the liturgy to its proper place among us. The Holy Spirit has inspired the Council

Fathers to propose certain changes in the Mass, but it will be carried into effect by men and women.

We should try to look upon the reform as a *challenge,* which we should accept with enthusiasm. Indeed, unless we are possessed of a certain degree of enthusiasm we shall not be able to set whole-heartedly about our task of implementing the reform. There are tremendous potentialities in the new form of the Mass. At the pastoral level these are of great importance. Priests will learn the great joy of having their people " with them " all the time at Mass. Active participation, which is one of the chief aims of the reform, will give satisfaction to both priest and people.

The Mass is one of our greatest treasures. It is no hidden or secret treasure, but one which must be brought more and more into the light, for all to view and admire and appreciate. It is to be hoped that slowly but surely, through the liturgical apostolate, the riches of the Mass will become evident to all.

The changes in the Mass, which have been introduced 7 March, 1965, are only a beginning. It is proposed to reform " the entire Order of the Mass " (Instruction, no. 48),[1] but this will be done gradually. We, too, must make a beginning of understanding the spirit and details of the reform. We will then see that the reform will have a definite influence on our spiritual lives. This is the ultimate aim of the changes: " to foster the formation of the faithful and that pastoral activity of which the liturgy is the summit and source ". (Instruction, no. 5.)

I wish to thank the Editor of the *Irish Ecclesiastical Record* for permission to use the translation of the Con-

---

[1] Whenever reference is made to the Instruction for the Proper Implementing of the Liturgy Constitution, the section is indicated as *no.* 1 etc. Whenever reference is made to the Constitution, the section is indicated as *art.* 1 etc.

stitution on the Sacred Liturgy made by Most Reverend Dr. Rodgers. I also wish to thank the Editor of *Doctrine and Life* for permission to make use of his translation of the Instruction for the Implementing of the Constitution, and for other material in *Vatican II: The Liturgy Constitution.*

I have drawn heavily on Dr. B. Fischer's booklet: *God's People about the Altar,* for my treatment of those parts of the Mass which belong to the people in Chapter 8.

There is one point on which I would like to forestall my critics. This book is essentially an attempt *to present* the problems of the new changes in the Mass. It does not claim *to solve* these problems. It is only time and experience that can provide us with solutions.

It will also be noticed that I have had to condense and compress a vast amount of information into a short space. This has been done on purpose, because what is needed by the busy priest and enquiring layman is a synthesis and a bird's-eye view. It would have made the book far too long had I indulged in analysis. Those who wish for more detailed information will find it in the books which I have listed in the bibliography.

DOM MARK TIERNEY, O.S.B.

PART I

THE CHALLENGE

CHAPTER I

VATICAN II AND PASTORAL PROBLEMS

It is surely a thought-provoking fact that Vatican II is the Church's twenty-first ecumenical Council. Whatever we may think of the Church's having reached her majority, everything points to her having entered a new era. The two words "maturity" and "responsibility" will appear from time to time in this book, for the Church today is seeking to instil these two factors into the hearts and minds of her faithful. The Church has accepted a challenge and she calls on all her sons and daughters to help her face it.

When Pope John XXIII decided to call a General Council, he did so for a very special reason. The Italian word "aggiornamento" sums up all that was in his mind at the time. He wished to bring about a renewal of Christian life in the world. In fact we can summarise the aims of the Second Vatican Council under four headings:

(i) To impart an ever-increasing vigour to the Christian life of the faithful;

(ii) To adapt and make more suitable to the needs of our age those institutions which are subject to change;

(iii) To foster whatever can promote union among all who believe in Christ;

(iv) To strengthen whatever can help to call all mankind into the Church's fold.

The underlying aim of the Council is seen to be

pastoral. In fact the whole Church is experiencing a great up-surge of pastoral activity and renewal. Every facet of the Church's life will be influenced in one way or other. Pope John went so far as to say that the Church was experiencing "a second Pentecost". Certainly the Holy Spirit is at work today in the Church, inspiring the Pope and the Council Fathers to bring about an "aggiornamento".

When the Council met on Monday, 22 October, 1962, the first schema presented to the Fathers for consideration was that on the Sacred Liturgy. This came as no surprise, for the liturgy was at the very centre of the Church's pastoral endeavour. Indeed, as Pope John said in his address, delivered on 8 December, 1962, at the closing of the first Session of Vatican II: "It was not by chance that the first schema to be considered was on the sacred Liturgy, which defines the relationship between man and God". And later, when he was promulgating the Constitution on the sacred Liturgy, Pope Paul said that "the liturgy was the first subject to be examined and the first, too, in a sense, in intrinsic worth and in importance for the life of the Church".

It is clear, therefore, that both Popes John and Paul, as well as the Council Fathers, realised the importance of the schema on the Liturgy for the re-vitalising of the Church's life today. They, therefore, gave their first attention to consider how the Liturgy might be brought into line with modern conditions and needs.

Here it may be as well to ponder on the contrast between the climate of the Council of Trent and that of Vatican II. At Trent the Church was clearly on the *defensive*. The Reformers made certain objections to which the Council had to give a reply; and their reply was given in firm and uncompromising formulae. During Vatican II, the Church is no longer on the defensive, but rather has she taken the *offensive*. The attendance at the Council of Protestant observers and the good-will displayed towards them and *vice versa*, are proof of the changed conditions between the 16th and 20th centuries.

In the 16th century the Church was trying to save her structure from being further undermined; she was trying to preserve intact whatever could be salvaged from the disasters of the Reformation crisis. In our own day the Church is more concerned with construction, with building-up, with re-newing. Pope John gave the lead in this, although the recent history of the Church in our time has witnessed a broadening of view on pastoral theology and pastoral methods. Thus it was that in 1955, the Sacred Congregation of Rites, when issuing its instructions for the proper carrying out of the restored Holy Week Rite, referred to the " pastoral purpose " of the new Ordo; they urged that the faithful be encouraged and instructed so that " they may take part in this celebration with intelligence and devotion ".

Again in 1957, Pope Pius XII, in his Motu Proprio *Sacram Communionem*, showed his pastoral concern by introducing a revolution in the laws governing the Eucharistic Fast. Pope Paul has made further relaxations in this law, to allow the maximum number of the faithful to participate fully in the Mass. Permission for evening Mass on Sunday, holydays and other occasions was likewise given for pastoral reasons.

The word *Pastoral* has a very wide significance. Briefly it may be defined as *having relation to the spiritual good of the people of God*. Anything, in other words, which works for the spiritual benefit of the Faithful comes under the heading of pastoral concern. Now it is a well-known fact that in many countries the bishops and clergy have in recent years been much perplexed by the falling off of the faithful in their practice of religion. In some cities in

Europe today, the number of practising Catholics is less than 40 per cent of the Catholic population. Two world wars and social and economic upheavals have been partly responsible for this sad state of affairs. But there are other reasons, and the Church has not hesitated to examine her own conscience and see if she has not been at fault in any way.

In France and Germany, since the war, various experiments were tried to enthuse the people to attend the Mass and other sacraments. The problem was a pastoral one: How to get the people to go to the Mass. Was there anything wrong with the way in which Mass was being celebrated? Did it have any real appeal for the people of the second half of the 20th century? Did it appear as something vital and necessary to the youth of our day? And so on. Such questions were asked, and some tentative solutions were tried. But none of them got to the heart of the matter. None of the experiments had sufficient backing to make any real impact.

In many countries, both in Europe and on the missions, it was felt that there was some "barrier" between the Mass and the people; and some of the most sincere of the critics stated categorically that this "barrier" was due to the language of the Mass. It was felt that the people would take more readily to the Mass, and the sacraments, if they were celebrated in the vernacular, in part, if not in whole.

The German, French, American and Irish hierarchies took a considerable step forward when they issued Rituals, allowing the use of the vernacular in parts of the Sacraments and in various Blessings. The *Collectio Rituum,* issued by the Irish bishops in 1960, is something which we can be very proud of, and already has given ample proof to the world that Ireland is not lagging behind other countries in opening up the riches of our Faith to the People of God. The Irish bishops allow the use of the vernacular so that "the people may have an understanding of the sacraments and their piety be aroused". Their motives are, therefore, clearly pastoral: the needs of the faithful.

Let us at this stage make one reflection: The pastoral concern of the Church in introducing the New Holy Week Ordo, in relaxing the Eucharistic Fast, in allowing the use of vernacular in the Sacraments and sacramentals, was bound to lead eventually to the application of these same principles to the Mass. These initial changes and adaptations were signs of further changes. Now that the Council has decided to introduce changes into the Mass, we must not show surprise or shock or alarm. Whatever changes come will be introduced slowly and carefully, with due allowance for human nature.

But perhaps what proved one of the most radical influences at the Council motivating change in the Church's liturgy was *the need of the missions*. After the loss of China to the Communist block, and with the disintegrating influence of the end of the colonial era in Africa, the Church found herself very much out of touch with the non-European way of life. Many missionary bishops, especially in Africa, India and Asia, were asking for a complete overhaul of liturgical practices, to suit the mental and cultural outlook of their peoples. Unless the Church allowed some relaxation and introduced changes, she might soon lose her already tenuous grip in foreign countries. First and foremost came the demand for more liberal use of the vernacular, but even more radical changes were suggested to suit non-European peoples. The Church, for pastoral reasons, could not turn her back on the young missionary communities.

The Church, it seemed, would have to adapt her liturgical worship to allow all men, of every race and colour, to shelter beneath her protecting wings. She must show herself as the Mother of all the People of God, not just of Europeans. This would, necessarily, entail change and adaptation. And in the last analysis it was found that some of the changes proposed for missionary countries might also be worth considering for the rest of the Church. Incidentally, during the Vatican Council, the voices of many missionary bishops reiterated these sentiments, and proposed unequivocally that changes should be made at once.

The same spirit was abroad in the Assisi Congress in 1956, when cardinals, bishops and scholars came together to formulate the principles on which any future liturgical reform should be based. It was mainly due to the work of men like Cardinal Lercaro and Father Jungmann that the Assisi Congress met with such a resounding success. And it was thanks to the foresight and understanding of Pope Pius XII that its proposals were given official recognition. Again and again at Assisi the speakers stressed the pastoral needs of the faithful. Father Jungmann could therefore state that " the interests of care of souls are again becoming the decisive factor—those pastoral interests, in other words, from which the forms of the liturgy had taken their origin in the early days of the Church . . ."

There are, in all these questions, three points of view which one may adopt. The first is that of the die-hards, the ultra conservatives, who maintain that the Church should make no change in her liturgical rites. They feel that age has lent a certain venerableness to the present forms of the Mass, sacraments and sacramentals. Was it to such as these that Pope John referred when he spoke of " those prophets of doom "?

At the opposite extreme we have those who would advocate change for any slight cause, change almost for mere change's sake. But here the pastoral rule of thumb will not hold out, and so their principles are unsound " pastorally " speaking.

There is, however, a middle course, which seems to be that taken by the majority of the Council Fathers, those whom one might call the moderate progressivists. These would have us introduce any necessary changes, provided they are warranted on pastoral grounds. And we shall see that it is on these very grounds that our recent changes have been introduced. This whole idea is well summed up by the Constitution:

> "There must be no innovations unless the good of the Church genuinely and certainly requires them, and care must be taken that any new forms adopted should in some way grow organically from forms already existing." (art. 23.)

The important part of this passage is the last. All changes must grow " organically " from forms already existing. The Mass is like a tree, whose trunk remains forever firm and strong, and whose roots are deeply embedded in the ground. But the branches and leaves may undergo some pruning, without in any way changing the " organic " structure of the tree. That is what the Church is doing at present, she is pruning the Mass, in order to give it new life, to make it more alive for us. She is doing this for Pastoral reasons, for the good of all the faithful.

CHAPTER II

THE BIBLICAL RENAISSANCE

The last fifty years or so have seen a great renaissance in biblical studies among Catholics. It used to be said that the Bible was a Protestant book. This is no longer the common viewpoint among Catholics. We have re-found the Bible, our most precious heritage and treasure. Articles 24 and 51 of the Constitution show how firmly the Bible is now rooted in our liturgical worship.

> " Sacred scripture is of the greatest importance in the celebration of the liturgy." (art. 24.)
>
> " The treasures of the Bible are to be opened up more lavishly, so that richer fare may be provided for the faithful at the table of God's word. In this way a more representative portion of the holy scriptures will be read to the people in the course of a prescribed number of years." (art. 51.)

It is certain that the Bible will be used more and more by Catholics in their public prayer, and both clergy and faithful will be called on to give it far closer study than formerly.

Indeed, here we find ourselves confronted with a very serious challenge, for on the whole it can be said that the Bible is an unknown quantity for most of us. In fact how many of us have made a personal study of the Bible and its contents? How many of us show any real interest in and concern for (not to mention love for) the Bible? Yet we admit that the Bible is the Word of God, that it is inspired, that it contains a spiritual message for us all. Surely there is something wrong here. We certainly don't lack the intelligence to understand the Bible. What we lack is incentive and a firm conviction that the Bible is *worth* reading.

Yet it will be quite impossible for us to enter into the spirit of the New Constitution unless we are prepared to give serious thought to the Bible and its message. The Bible is the very foundation of our Faith and it is the great source book of the Liturgy. It is a veritable mine of spiritual learning and inspiration, not to speak of prayer. For after all, the Psalms are part of the Bible.

What we have to do is to take some action. There are some excellent books to help us read the Bible, such as Fr. Daniel E. Lupton's two small volumes,[1] Fr. McKenzie's classical book *The Two-Edged Sword,* and Fr. Moriarty's *Introduction to the Old Testament*. Perhaps the Old Testament will be our real problem, although we should not take it for granted that we are all that familiar with the New Testament. Fr. Patrick Fannon's book on *The Four Gospels* and Fr. Blenkinsopp's *Corinthian Mirror* are up-to-date studies worth reading.

What has prevented our entering into the world of the Bible up to this has been the illusion that we can read the sacred books as they stand. We forget that their message is hidden in a maze of semitic thought and language, and we must first study the world of the Bible if we are to make it really our own.[2] It will take some courage, deter-

---

[1] *A Guide to Reading the Bible* (Sheed & Ward). Also to be recommended is the excellent book by Fr. Bruce Vawter: *A Path Through Genesis.* (Sheed & Ward.)

[2] Cf. Anderson: *The Living World of the Old Testament* (Longmans).

mination and perseverance; but it will enrich our spiritual life, our preaching or teaching, and will help us to understand the Liturgy in a way never possible before.

Let us be convinced that there has been such a thing as a biblical renaissance. The work of the best scholars is now at our door-step, written in non-technical language. We are not going to be asked to learn Hebrew or even Greek. But we are asked to try to study the Hebrew and Greek cultures and mentalities. If both the clergy and faithful fail to draw upon the great treasures of biblical lore uncovered these past fifty years, they will be out of step with the rest of the Church. We must fall in line with the main stream of Church endeavour, and accept the free gift of the mental efforts of our French and German fellow Catholics. Naturally we must adapt the details of our interpretation to our needs, but for the most part the message of the Bible is a universal message, valid for all peoples and for all times.

By studying the Bible in the light of modern research, our minds will not only be able to understand the context, but also the content of the Word of God. Now that the Homily at Mass has been restored to its rightful place in our public worship, both clergy and faithful will require a keener sense of Scripture than before. The Bible will be seen as Sacred History, the History of Salvation, working out God's designs in a mysterious but providential way. The Jews will be seen as The Chosen People of God, whose rites and beliefs and history have a meaning for 20th century Christians. Catholics will no longer imagine that they can fulfil their Sunday obligation by arriving in time for the Offertory. The division of the Mass into *The Liturgy of the Word* and *The Liturgy of the Eucharist*, and the urgent appeal to the faithful to participate fully in both parts, will call for a new appreciation of the Bible.

In monastic tradition the Bible was called " divine reading " (Lectio divina). The monks were required to spend several hours each day in sacred reading, outside choir. But it was always felt that the Bible was especially canonised and made live when it formed part of liturgical prayer. And indeed it is in the context of the liturgy that the Bible received its authentic interpretation and emphasis, so that the phrase was coined " the rule of prayer is the rule of believing " (Lex orandi, lex credendi). As the Church prays, so does she believe. If the Church celebrates the Feast of Christ's Nativity, it is simply because she believes in the fact of Christ's Birth at Bethlehem. And the Church has always taken great care to insert in the liturgy of each feast those biblical texts which are most relevant to it. In other words, the Bible is often interpreted in the light of its liturgical setting and vice versa. As Cardinal Bea said at the Assisi Congress in 1956 " the congregation of the faithful which gathers together for the celebration of the eucharistic sacrifice is the most auspicious place for the reading and fruitful explanation of the Word of God ".

The Bible is not just any book, not just a precious relic of the past, not even just a best-seller; it is the Word of God. It is not only the Gospel that is " the Good News ", the whole Bible contains a message, an essential message for us all. And the proclamation of the Word of God has always been considered as a sacred action, an encounter with God. Hence it is that the deacon incenses the Gospel

Book before singing the Gospel, and the celebrant kisses the Book afterwards. It is Christ who speaks to us in the Gospel, and becomes present again among us.

Finally, with the introduction of the vernacular into the readings from Scripture at Mass, we will be faced with a more vivid realisation of the message of the Bible. The Bible should become more alive, and this will call for greater care on the part of the person reading the passages in public. It will also call for a new approach to the using of missals by the faithful, who should be encouraged to listen, rather than follow in their missals, while the Epistle and Gospel are being read aloud. Just as the principle has been put forward in the new Instruction that the Celebrant should not read what another minister is reading, in like manner the faithful should be instructed in the art of listening to the Word of God being both read and explained to them. This is a definite challenge to us all, readers, preachers and hearers of the Word of God. The very simplicity of the language and thought of the Bible is often deceptive; yet it is pure gold and must be given to the faithful in its pristine beauty.

CHAPTER III

THE CATECHETICAL RENEWAL

The Church is very much concerned about getting her message across to modern man. The methods and approach of former days will call for some adaptation. She must preach the Good News to living men, and her words must be " alive " to her listeners. In recent years we have seen a considerable step forward in catechetical instruction. It is now realised that catechetics are not simply for children, but also for adults, and new methods have been worked out for teaching and preaching to men, women and children.

If we are to put ourselves in line with the rest of the Church in this matter, we shall have to re-examine our whole approach to catechetics. Again this is a challenge to us all, clergy, religious and laity. It is not a question of the clergy preparing a sugar-coated pill for the faithful to swallow. Catechesis is something dynamic, necessary, essential for the full flowering of Christian life at every stage of our Christian development. It will involve the providing of both a formation and information; it will mean the calling on the Holy Spirit to instruct and guide our ministry; it will call for a new approach to preaching the Gospel. Our understanding of the Mass and the Sacraments will be enriched if we base it on an authentic catechesis. Pastoral liturgy and catechetics, along with the study of the Bible, will provide the basic structure of our Christian life.

Although all this will call for a new approach, it is in fact a return to the authentic sources of religious pedagogy. Modern catechetics has the task of making the Christian message intelligent and alive for 20th century men and women. All outmoded ways of thought, all antiquated formulae, will have to be discarded. It will call for much psychological insight on the part of the teacher or preacher, who will adapt his words to the age, mentality and understanding of his audience.

One of the principles we must accept is this: " The adult is always the subject of catechesis " (Coudreau). The child remains in catechism class for a number of years, but he has assimilated the Faith with a child mind. If he is to be a fully-fledged, adult, mature, responsible Christian, he will have to come to grips with the problems of Faith at an adult level. The Faith must not appear as something remote, or even of class-room interest, for him. He must constantly see it as a call, as a demand, as a challenge. Too often Faith has been looked at from the mere point of an act of Faith, and not rather as *a way of life*. Living the Faith is not just a nice phrase, but a very real thing.

Perhaps, the real trouble is that we who live in a Christian country do not find ourselves called upon to give witness to our Faith. The only way we feel that catechetics enter into our life is in the form of the Decalogue. We must keep the Ten Commandments, and in doing this we are proving ourselves practical Christians. Morality is, of course, something which we hold very dear, but any negative approach to morality will fail in its object. Catechetics must relate morality to Faith, must see the working of the Spirit in every baptised Christian. And the Liturgy will be found as much a source of teaching catechetics as the Ten Commandments.

Our modern catechetics will provide an essential synthesis for all our thinking and teaching about religion. It will mean providing a wider programme, with new directions. Yet, basically, our teaching will be the same as that which St. Peter provided on Pentecost day for his listeners in Jerusalem. It was very simple: "Repent and be baptized, every one of you, in the name of Jesus Christ, to have your sins forgiven; then you will receive the gift of the Holy Spirit. This promise is for you and for your children, and for all those, however far away, whom the Lord our God calls to himself. . . And he used many more words besides, *urgently appealing to them*". That is what our catechesis should be: "an urgent appeal". We must make it sound real, make it sound attractive, make it appealing. It would be a disservice to the Word of God did we preach it nonchalantly, carelessly, with a half-hearted conviction in our voice and manner.

But likewise, the Church now calls upon her faithful to take a greater interest in understanding the message of God. Vatican II has not just issued directives for the clergy. Its appeal has been made to all. This is necessary because the Church uses so many signs and symbols in her worship, that even the Mass itself cannot be understood unless the meaning of these signs and symbols are pointed out to us. And this can only be done if we are prepared to take some trouble, to read about our faith, to study it, and come to grips with its content.

Our catechesis will, of course, be based upon the Bible and the Liturgy. It will entail the explanation of such key-concepts as Church "covenant", "alliance", "witness", "sacrament", "mystery", etc. We shall try to relate our teaching to prayer, and to impress upon our listeners that silence and recollection are very necessary if our prayer-life is to develop and thrive. We shall not be content with relating simple bible stories, but rather we must present the Bible message as part of God's revelation, as His saving word. And above all we shall show in what manner we can participate in the sacred events related in the Bible; for the Liturgy re-lives these events in the course of each year. Ultimately it will be evident that the liturgical year presents us with a means of drawing life from the celebration of the sacred mysteries of Christ's life. The Liturgy brings us into direct contact with Christ. The Mass must be seen as *the* Christ-encounter *par excellence*.

It is for this very purpose that the Instruction of 26 September 1964 states that " it is especially necessary that there be a close union between the liturgy and catechesis, religious formation, and preaching ". (No. 7.) We are all called upon, therefore, to study the norms of the catechetical renewal, and to use whatever modern methods are recommended in our communicating the faith and divine life to others.

CHAPTER IV

THE LITURGICAL REVIVAL

When speaking of the liturgical movement which the Catholic world has witnessed during the past fifty years or so, the word "revival" is usually the term used. This is an important point, because it stresses the fact that the movement is not just some modern craze or innovation, but a genuine return to traditional forms of worship. In fact there was a time in the 1920's and 1930's when liturgists were rather frowned upon and considered as a group of eccentrics, who had more than one bee in their collective bonnet. Perhaps some enthusiasts did go too far in their experimentation, but on the whole the liturgical movement has been marked by restraint. The liturgical movement is marked especially by its pastoral concern.

Let us first of all have a look at the word " liturgical ". It comes from the Greek word *leitourgia,* which means Public Service. In ancient Greece anyone who donated money to erect a public building, or who endowed a library for public use, was considered as performing a public service. In fact any act which benefited one's fellow citizens was called by this term leitourgia. The Church soon adopted the term to cover all forms of public worship, maintaining that prayer for mankind was the highest form of public service possible. And so the term "Liturgy" came into our Christian vocabulary. It covers not only the Mass, but the other sacraments as well, the sacramentals, the Divine Office, the Liturgical Year, sacred music and sacred art. All these subjects are dealt with by the new Constitution on the Liturgy.

It would be out of place here to attempt even a summary of the historical development of the liturgical revival. What is more to the point for our purpose is to draw the main lines of thought which governed it. In fact the Constitution draws these lines for us, when laying down the principles for the restoration and promotion of the sacred liturgy.

The first principle, and the most important one, is that which concerns the active participation of the faithful in the public worship of the Church: *The faithful have a right and duty to participate actively in the Mass.* There is no denying the fact that the Mass had become too much the concern of the clergy, with the faithful playing a silent and purely passive rôle. The faithful were supposed to "assist *at* Mass", "to attend Mass", "to be present *at* Mass". One of the chief results of the liturgical revival has been the stressing of the active rôle of the faithful. Liturgists have studied the more ancient forms of Mass and have found that from the earliest days of Christianity the faithful took a clear and active part in it. It has come as no surprise, therefore, to find the Constitution making the following point:

> "Mother Church earnestly desires that all the faithful should be led to that full, conscious and active participation in liturgical celebrations which is demanded by the very nature of the liturgy. Such participation by the Christian people as a 'chosen race, a royal priesthood, a holy nation, a redeemed people' is their right and duty by reason of their baptism. In the restoration and promotion of the sacred liturgy, the full and active participation by all the people is the aim to be considered before all else . . ." (art. 14)

If this active participation of the faithful is to be carried to its logical and complete conclusion, it will call for a change of mind among us all. And the whole basis for this change of mind will be an understanding of our share in the priesthood of Christ. By quoting the Epistle of St. Peter: " You are a chosen race, *a royal priesthood,* a holy nation ", the Constitution wishes to remind us that by our baptism we have been given a share in Christ's priesthood. It is not only the bishops and priests of the Church who are dedicated to God, although they alone have the power to change bread and wine into the Body and Blood of Christ. Every baptised Christian has the power to *offer up* sacrifice, to share in the prayer of the community. For ultimately all prayer is offered to God by the community, and we pray as " the people of God ", as the holy people of God (Plebs sancta). The faithful exercise their priesthood to the most excellent degree when they come to Mass and join in the great action which is both a sacrament and sacrifice. It will entail joining in the prayers, giving their vocal assent to the readings and chants, offering the Mass along with the priest, and participating in the sacrifice by receiving Holy Communion during it.

Therefore, we must conclude that the first-fruits of the liturgical revival have been the stressing of this basic idea of full, active participation of the faithful in the public worship of the Church. It is both *a fact* and *a right. The fact* has been proved historically and theologically, based on the shared priesthood of Christ by all baptised persons, and on the beliefs and practices of the early days of the Church. *The right* has yet to be asserted and exercised by the faithful. This will only come with time. We must be convinced that every Christian has a right and a duty to take part actively in the public worship of the Church, and that this right is no mere usurpation, but a sacred duty.

The second principle follows from the first and lays down the manner and fashion of this active participation by the faithful. The Constitution makes the following statement:

> "The Church, therefore, earnestly desires that those who have faith in Christ, when present at this mystery of Faith, should not be there as *strangers or silent spectators;* on the contrary, through an adequate understanding of the rites and prayers they should take part in the sacred action conscious of what they are doing, with devotion and full collaboration. They should be instructed by God's word and be nourished at the table of the Lord's body; they should give thanks to God; by offering the immaculate victim not only through the hands of the priest, but also with him, they should learn to offer themselves. . ." (art. 48)

This article shows the multiple way in which the faithful may take an active part in the Mass. They are to come to Mass to be nourished (i) by the word of God, read for them; (ii) by the Lord's body, distributed to them. They are to come to Mass to give thanks to God, through Christ, for the Redemption. And they are to offer "the immaculate victim not only through the hands of the priest, but also with him. . ." Yes, the faithful are now clearly told by the Constitution that they can and should offer Mass, with and through the priest. And finally they are called upon to offer themselves. The Mass, though a communal and corporate act, is also of benefit to us as individuals. Each one of us must offer himself at Mass, along with Christ, as victim to the eternal Father.

It follows from all this that there are, in fact, three basic ways of actively participating in the liturgy (i) internal participation (ii) external participation and (iii) sacramental sharing. *Internal participation* is the most elemental and essential form, assuring a personal commitment to and interest in public worship. *External participation* involves our giving outward expression to our internal dispositions, through acts of adoration, thanksgiving, reparation. This is done through certain gestures, attitudes of the body, by using our voice in song and speech. Finally our *sacramental sharing* is achieved by partaking in the sacrificial meal, by receiving Holy Communion. The liturgical revival has taught us that full, active participation in the Mass calls for a putting into practice of the three forms as outlined above. The Constitution has canonised them, and made them the basis for the reform of the liturgy. (art. 19)

The third principle which we would propose relates to the function of the People of God as "the Assembly": *The assembly of the People of God at Mass is a sacred sign, manifesting the Church of God on earth, and assuring the presence of Christ in their midst.* By our birth we are born into a human family; by our baptism we are born into the family of God. The first birth gives us a right to join in all the social and communal activities of our family-life; the second gives us the right to join in all the community acts of the Church of God. As members of a human family we merge our individuality, by adding our personal effort to the common endeavour; likewise in our liturgical worship we merge our individuality in the great common prayer to God, raised by the Church on behalf of all her children.

All this is summed up by the Constitution in the following words:

> "Liturgical services are not private functions, but are celebrations of the Church, which is the 'sacrament of unity'—namely the holy people united and ordered under their bishops.
>
> "Therefore liturgical services pertain to the whole body of the Church; they manifest it and have effect upon it; but they concern the individual members of the Church in different ways, according to their different rank, office and activity." (art. 26)

It will be seen that there are different functions to be fulfilled by the different members of the assembly. There is the celebrant, who presides; then the servers, lectors, commentators and members of the choir, who "also exercise a genuine liturgical function" (art. 29); and finally the people, who "should be encouraged to take part by means of acclamations, responses, psalmody, antiphons and hymns, as well as by actions, gestures, and bodily attitudes". (Art. 30.) Certainly "the liturgy makes distinctions between persons according to their liturgical function and clerical rank" (art. 32), but all the ministers are at the service of the assembly. It is the latter that counts most of all. *It is the assembly which gives public expression to the presence of the Church.* (art. 27) When we come to Mass, therefore, we must not see ourselves as isolated individuals, praying apart, for ourselves, by ourselves. Rather, we should come to worship, conscious that we are about to make up the Assembly of the people of God, and that our prayer is to be offered by an accredited minister of Christ, on our behalf and on behalf of the whole Church; and that the sacrifice which we offer is offered by the whole assembly. Unless we appreciate this important fact, our worship will lose much of its richness and meaning.

We therefore come to realise that "the Mass is never to be considered as a merely clerical performance of a mysterious rite at which the people are only silent spectators". (Howell) All are sharers in the covenant; all are asked to fulfil their part of the alliance. We Catholics believe in the visible Church, manifested here on earth, and made present most especially during the celebration of the Eucharist. And the Church of Christ is made visible in the assembly when each member actively shares in the public worship, by fulfilling that function which is his by reason of his baptism.

The liturgical revival has not only restored to the people of God their proper place in the celebration of the Mass, but it has also given us a deeper understanding of the structure of the Mass. And thus it is possible to draw a fourth principle which will be one of the bases for the new changes in the Mass: The Mass comprises two essential parts: (i) The liturgy of the Word (ii) the liturgy of the Eucharist. This new outlook has restored to the first part of the Mass its rightful and traditional place and dignity. We must be prepared to see the liturgy of the Word even still more expanded, with perhaps longer or several passages from scripture, instead of just the Epistle and Gospel.

In fact, of course, as the Constitution says: "The two parts are so closely connected with each other that they form but one single act of worship. Accordingly, this sacred Synod strongly urges pastors of souls that, when instructing the faithful, they insistently teach them to take their part in the entire Mass, especially on Sundays and holidays of obligation." (art. 56)

But what is more to our purpose is the fact that the first part of the Mass, the liturgy of the Word, will change our very conception of the priest at the altar, offering sacrifice all the time. The function of the celebrant at this stage will be to break the bread of the word of God so that the congregation may partake of it. Later on, in the second part of the Mass, they will be invited to partake of the eucharistic Bread, which the priest has already broken for them.

Finally, the liturgical revival has taught us that the liturgy is not just a matter of rubrics and ceremonial. Rubrics and ceremonial are necessary parts of the liturgical celebrations; they are, as it were the icing round the cake, but they are not the cake itself. "The liturgy is the summit towards which the activity of the Church is directed: at the same time it is the fount from which all her power flows.

For the aim and object of apostolic work is that all who are made sons of God by faith and baptism should come together to praise God in the midst of his Church, to take part in the sacrifice and to eat the Lord's supper."(Const. art. 10.)

By the liturgy " grace is poured forth upon us; and the sanctification of men in Christ and the glorification of God, to which all other activities of the Church are directed as towards their end, is achieved in the most efficacious possible way." (*ibid.*) The liturgy is the continuation of the work of Christ, a carrying out of his great acts of redemption by sacred actions. It is the daily application of the graces of the redemption to all mankind. It is the re-living " in mystery " of Christ's Passion, Death and glorification. The liturgy is the life of the Church, making present again the glorified Christ.

And so the Constitution gives us this final principle concerning the liturgy:

> " *Every liturgical celebration,* because it is an action of Christ the priest and of his body which is the Church, *is a sacred action surpassing all others;* no other action of the Church can equal its efficiency by the same title and to the same degree." (art. 7)

We have, therefore, ample and multiple reasons for accepting the dignity and necessity of liturgical celebrations. It is the focal point of all our prayer, the main-spring of our spiritual nourishment, the constant means of communicating with God.

PART II

THE ENCOUNTER

CHAPTER V

GENERAL PRINCIPLES OF CHANGE

(i) *There are certain changeable elements in the Mass.*

The Constitution states that "the liturgy is made up of unchangeable elements divinely instituted and of elements subject to change. These latter not only may be changed, but *ought to be changed* with the passage of time, if they have suffered from the intrusion of anything out of harmony with the inner nature of the liturgy or have become unsuited to it". (art. 21)

These words are but an echo of those written by Pope Pius XII in *Mediator Dei:* "The sacred liturgy includes divine as well as human elements. The former, as is clear, cannot be changed in any way by men, since they were instituted by the Divine Redeemer. But the latter admit of various modifications as the needs of the age, circumstances, and men require and which the ecclesiastical hierarchy, under the guidance of the Holy Spirit, approves". (art. 54)

It is clear from all this that when we come to discuss changes in the Mass, such changes

(i) will only concern *the human elements*

(ii) will be in fact *modifications*

(iii) will be introduced by *ecclesiastical authority*

(iv) will be a sign of *growth and vitality.*

Fr. Jungmann already made this quite clear at Assisi in 1956 when he said that "the liturgy is like a tree, which has grown in the changing climate of world history, and which has experienced stormy as well as flourishing times. Its real growth, however, comes from within, from those life forces whence it took its origin." "The Mass", continues Fr. Jungmann, " is a precious gift, treasured by the Church with reverence through the centuries. But the Church has not merely preserved and guarded this treasure, she has also developed it and embellished it with rich forms ".

Liturgical scholars assure us that the Mass has changed considerably in its external forms from time to time. Even the name " Mass " has not always been in use. " The breaking of bread " (Act. ii), " The Lord's Supper " (I Cor. xi. 20), " The Eucharist " (Didaché), " The Offering " (our Irish An tAifreann), have all been used at one time or another. We have only to reflect on the difference between the Roman and Eastern rites of celebrating Mass to realise just how far *external changes* can go.

It would be contrary to the known fact to assert that the Mass should be, or could be, " freezed ". Although we have seen very few changes in the Mass since Pope Pius V's reform of 1570, there have been reasons for this " static " state of affairs. And it is this very " static " element which is now deplored. The Constitution on the sacred liturgy has introduced changes into the human elements in the Mass; the divinely-instituted elements have been left unchanged.

(ii) *A sound tradition should be retained.*

One of the guiding principles behind the liturgical reform is the desire to return to a more authentic tradition in our public worship. The Constitution calls for a " careful investigation, based on theological, historical and pastoral grounds, to be made into each part of the liturgy which is to be revised ". (art. 23)

It must be quite evident that the Church is not setting about " inventing " new forms of worship. She is concerned with restoring and reviving the best traditions which scholars have unearthed for her. We must not imagine that this has been suddenly sprung upon the Church. Work has been going on for over fifty years and we are only now reaping the fruit of the labours of men like Dom Lambert Beauduin.

There is, in fact, a serious, genuine and reliable basis for such a return to ancient practices. History, theology and pastoral care will be all summoned to play a part in gauging the actual changes to be introduced. The Constitution assures us that "parts which with the passage of time came to be duplicated, or were added with little advantage, are to be omitted. Other parts, which suffered loss through accidents of history are to be restored to the vigour they had *in the days of the holy Fathers*, as may seem useful and necessary." (art. 50)

Thus it is that while safeguarding faithfully the substance of the Mass-rite, it is legitimate to make certain changes which will serve some useful purpose, or which are necessary. Because the Mass in its present form is somewhat complicated, it is of pastoral utility that some simplifications and adaptations be made. The numerous genuflections of the celebrant, the multiple signs of the Cross, kisses of the altar, etc are difficult to explain and it seems useful to reduce them in number.

It is the aim of the Constitution that the Mass become once more a simple rite, as it was in the early days of the Church. It is certain that the traditional form of worship was both simple and easy to follow: the Mass was a sacrificial meal, a sacred banquet, in which all the faithful took part. It is not intended to restore the whole past way of celebrating Mass, but to retain only the best traditions which we can discern. It is not necessary to add that this process of adaptation and restoration will take a long time to complete. The changes will only be introduced slowly and after much mature deliberation.

(iii) *The faithful should be able to understand and participate.*

Underlying all the changes in the Mass is the double aim of the Constitution:

(i) to foster the formation of the faithful and

(ii) to guarantee that pastoral activity of which the liturgy is the summit and source. (art. 5)

Present pastoral needs must dictate and guide the changes made. Therefore, while the Constitution concerns itself about ceremonial and the external rite of worship, it is primarily interested in developing those internal, personal and communal elements in the liturgy which touch the faithful. It is desired that the people of God worship in a more fitting and beneficial manner.

No one can deny that the Mass had become divorced from its original form, with the faithful mere onlookers, and the priest celebrating Mass " for " them. Communal worship had been lost sight of. It was for this very reason that that Constitution declared: " Whenever rites, according to their specific nature, make provision for communal celebration involving the presence and active participation of the faithful, it is to be stressed that in so far as it is possible this method of celebrating them is to be preferred to a celebration that is individual and quasi-private." (art. 27) The rubrics of the present Roman rite hardly ever mention the people. A considerable break-through was made in the restored rite for Holy Week, when the faithful were encouraged to take part in the renewal of their baptismal vows, to join in the Palm Sunday procession, to recite the Our Father on Good Friday, etc. All future amendments of the rubrics will make reference to the faithful and provide for their participating in the Church's worship.

The Constitution considers all this with a certain urgency, and especially lays emphasis on the rôle of the liturgy in the spiritual formation of the faithful. "The liturgy is the summit towards which the activity of the Church is directed . . . the fount from which all her power flows" (art. 10). "But in order that the liturgy may be able to produce its full effects it is necessary that the faithful come to it with proper dispositions, that their minds should be attuned to their voices, and that they should co-operate with heavenly grace less they receive it in vain. Pastors of souls must, therefore, realise that, when the liturgy is celebrated, something more is required than the laws governing valid and lawful celebration. It is their duty also to ensure that *the faithful take part fully aware of what they are doing, actively engaged in the rite and enriched by it.*" (art. 11)

The changes which will take place in the Mass-rite will enable the Church's worship to be more easily understood by the faithful. They will be "distinguished by a noble simplicity". (art. 34) The ceremonies, actions, readings, etc., will be marked by their shortness and clarity. "They should be within the people's powers of comprehension and normally should not require much explanation." (*ibid.*) The principle here in question is the intelligibility of the various rites and ceremonies, which have not always been within the easy comprehension of the faithful. There is a need for reform here, and it is certain that in the days to come the liturgy will have a far greater impact upon the people than hitherto. "The Christian people, as far as possible, should be able to understand them with ease and take part in them fully, actively, and as is proper to a community." (art. 21)

The liturgy is to be the chief means whereby the faithful are to be formed spiritually. The pastoral importance of the liturgical celebrations and the opportunities which they provide for deepening the faith of the people are stressed by the Council. "Even though the liturgy is not the whole of the Church's activity, great care must be taken that pastoral work be properly linked with it . . . Bishops and their helpers in the priesthood should set great store by their whole liturgy-centred apostolate. Thus the faithful too, by perfect participation in the liturgy, will receive the divine life abundantly and, having become Christ's leaven and the salt of the earth, *they* will announce and transmit it to others." (Instruction, arts. 7 and 8) This last sentence is unique, for it shows how much the mind of the Church is directed towards producing a mature and responsible laity, who will announce and transmit the message of Christianity to others. The Instruction goes on to say that it is the rôle of lay associations "to share more intimately in the life of the Church and to assist pastors in organising the liturgical life of the parish". (art. 19)

This principle, therefore, makes it quite clear that the faithful must take part in the Mass by an intelligent understanding of the sacred ceremonies and by actively participating in them. Mere "passive" attendance at Mass will no longer be the normal thing. The Church is giving the faithful a *total* view of the liturgy in this matter, demanding an internal and an external involvement. Obviously not all will have the same level of understanding, just as not all will be able to contribute to the external participation equally. The Church sets out the ideal to be aimed at; but permits and accepts different levels of achievement.

(iv) *The Reform covers all the Mass.*

Although the implementation of the Constitution will mean the detailing of separate items in the Mass-liturgy, the reform is essentially to affect the whole Mass. We shall consider in a later chapter the actual changes. Here it is a question of stating a general principle. The Mass is now shown to consist of two parts: the Liturgy of the Word and the Eucharistic Liturgy, which form two parts of one single act of worship. The Mass is, therefore, shown to be both word and sacrament-sacrifice. The Constitution aims at restoring a proper *balance* in the Mass. The Mass is seen as the occasion when the faithful are " instructed by God's word and nourished at the table of the Lord's Body ". (art. 48)

In this way, the Church will forestall any critics who may accuse her of just tampering with the Mass. The spirit of the new reform is not just the result of attention to detail. It goes beyond the separate changes. The liturgy is shown as something which is suited to man in his present state. It is sacramental, it uses symbols, and it re-enacts in mystery the Passion, Death, Resurrection and exaltation of Christ. The Constitution makes it quite clear that its immediate goal is the Sunday Mass. " Efforts must be made to encourage a sense of community within the parish, above all in the common celebration of the Sunday Mass." (art. 49) The Mass is seen as a community act and the Sunday parish Mass or Masses will be greatly enriched by a worthy carrying out of the injunctions laid down by the Constitution. The Sunday Mass is seen as the celebration of the Paschal Mystery, that is, the Passion, Death and glorification of Christ. Each community of worshippers fulfils its rôle in the Church by participating in common, in an active way, in the great public act of worship to God.

When the reforms are completed we should have a deeper understanding of the Mass. We should certainly have a deeper sense of being a community when we worship together. We shall likewise see the Mass a whole, composed, no doubt, of several parts, but being nonetheless a unity. The Constitution is concerned to assist the faith and piety of the people. It makes very little allowance for the celebrant, who is required to accommodate himself to the needs of his congregation. The Constitution has tapped the hidden resources of the Mass, has outlined the rôle of the celebrant by detailing the parts which belong to him; and it has furthermore given back to the faithful those parts which belonged to them by right. In readjusting the balance in the Mass the Constitution has given us an opportunity of entering more fully than ever into the spirit of the liturgy. It has restored

(i) the Mass as the centre of Christian worship,

(ii) the liturgy of the Word to its rightful place

(iii) the sense of community among the faithful at Mass.

It would therefore be wrong to imagine that the changes in the Mass are meant to be taken simply in their isolated units. The various changes are important, of course, in their own way. But the overall look at these changes must bring us to see the Mass in a new light. It is the whole Mass which has been changed, or rather new emphases have been given to the Mass in its structural, doctrinal, and liturgical lay-out. All this will call for mental adaptation on our part.

CHAPTER VI

LIVING LANGUAGES IN THE MASS

It is just ten years since Cyril Korolevsky, a priest of the Byzantine rite, wrote a book called *Living Languages in Catholic Worship*. In this book he illustrated the historical factors in both the East and West which have resulted in what we call " the problem of the vernacular ". The author has one telling passage which is worth quoting:

> " The liturgy is the Church's true common prayer, and it is meant for everybody, not for the clergy alone. The people can take part in it to the full only if they understand it; and not everybody can afford to buy a bilingual Missal, or has the ability and education necessary for the proper use of it. Quite involuntarily, the community of faithful is split between two categories; those, generally the economically better off, who have some classical culture and can understand and appreciate the Roman liturgy, and those who do not understand it properly and have no means of doing so." (p. 164)

It is first of all necessary to ask ourselves the question: Does the actual language used in the Mass make a difference to those participating? In other words, has the use of Latin been a help or a hindrance towards a fruitful participation in the Mass? These questions came up for consideration when the Fathers of the Council were discussing article 54 of the Constitution on the Sacred Liturgy. No categorical answer was given one way or another. Language was admitted to be a means of communication between people; furthermore, the Mass is a dialogue between God and His people and the people must give their assent to the prayers and sacred rites. From this it followed that some use of the vernacular would be helpful, for pastoral reasons, to assist the faith and piety of the people. And as the principle was established that certain parts of the Mass belong to the people, these parts should be said by them in a language which they can understand. It is noteworthy that " however great may be the need of the clergy for the same concession, the primary consideration is that of the faithful ". (McManus)

The Constitution first of all lays down the principle that " the use of the Latin language, with due respect to particular law, is to be preserved in the Latin rites ". (art. 36) Commenting on this point Fr. Braga says that Latin is to be retained because it serves " as a sign of unity ". It is certainly this, as any priest can bear out who has travelled abroad. No matter where we go, we find a missal and a Mass rite in Latin which we can use. Catholic priests can travel anywhere in the world and not be inconvenienced by any language barrier.

On the other hand it is likewise admitted by the Council that some use of the vernacular is desirable: " But since the use of the vernacular whether in the Mass, the administration of the sacraments or in other parts of the liturgy, may frequently *be of great advantage to the people,* a wider use may be made of it, especially in readings and directives, in some prayers and chants." (art. 36) " It is, however, for the competent territorial ecclesiastical authority to decide whether, and to what extent, the vernacular language is to be used." (*ibid.*) Those parts of the Mass which are recommended as more suitable in the vernacular are the ones which are directed towards the instruction of the people (readings) or else are said or sung by them (prayers and chants). It is evident, says Fr. Braga, that the Council Fathers were impelled by pastoral motives to allow such use of the vernacular in the Mass.

It is for this reason that the Constitution in art. 54 states that " a suitable place *may be found* for the vernacular in Masses which are celebrated with the people ". The original draft of the Constitution had the words " should be " instead of " may be found ", but this was changed after the debate in order to leave complete liberty to the territorial authorities who are competent to make this decision. (McManus)

There will be much speculation about the actual meaning of the words " missa cum populo ". The Council's concession of the vernacular for Mass would seem to cover every case except that in which a priest was celebrating Mass with only a server present. Nothing is said in the Constitution with regard to the size of the congregation or the circumstances (McManus). Fr. Braga states simply that Latin is to be retained in those cases where individual priests say Mass privately (*In Missis ergo quae privatim a singulis sacerdotibus celebrantur lingua latina servabitur*). From all this it follows that the use of the vernacular is permitted in cases where only a few people are present. " There is nothing whatever in the Constitution to suggest that the concession is limited to the regularly scheduled Masses, the parish Mass, the community Mass, or the like." (McManus)

It is interesting to note that " no part of the Mass *per se* is excluded from the concession of using the vernacular ". (Braga) However, the Constitution details those parts which are more suitable: " as local conditions may warrant, in those parts which pertain to the people " (art. 5.4) the vernacular may be used. This latter phrase " which pertain to the people " requires close attention. First of all we must beware of imagining that the Council intended that the first part of the Mass, i.e. the Liturgy of the Word, should be entirely in the vernacular, while the second part, i.e. the Liturgy of the Eucharist, should be in Latin. For art. 33 states that " the people reply to God both by song and prayer ", and already we have seen that such songs and prayers will be in the vernacular. (art. 36) Hence we come to the conclusion that the Council sees a *didactic* element in other parts of the Mass than the readings.

Secondly, we must not be led to think that those parts of the Mass which are said in the mother-tongue are *secondary,* while those said in Latin are of prime importance. It is true that the Canon and central part of the Mass remain in Latin. But the Mass is a unity, and the only reason why the vernacular is introduced is to allow the people to participate in it with greater piety, devotion and understanding. As art. 30 says: " To promote active participation, the people should be encouraged to take part by means of acclamations, responses, psalms, antiphons, hymns, etc." Those parts which pertain to the people are important, because they give the faithful an opportunity of joining in the Mass, and offering it more fully, along with the priest.

Thirdly, the use of the vernacular will help to give a sense of community to the congregation present. While it is true that at each Mass it is the whole Church which is at prayer, nonetheless, each separate congregation forms a cell of the whole Church, and must pray in unity. The common bond of language will give unison to their prayer, and permit all to join in with understanding and devotion. The people of God should never feel " strangers " in the House of God. The use of the vernacular will help to make them feel more at home there. Therefore, we see that the Constitution is legislating for individual communities of worshippers, and in so far as the use of the mother-tongue will weld them into a community and give them a sense of unity, it will serve the purpose intended by the Council Fathers.

The details of the occasions when the vernacular may be used at Mass are given in the Instruction no. 57.

CHAPTER VII

THE CHANGES IN THE MASS

While the Constitution lays down the general principles upon which all reform will be based, it is in the document entitled " Instruction by the Sacred Congregation of Rites on the Proper Implementing of the Liturgy Constitution " that we find the details of the actual changes in the Mass. It is worth noting that the changes will be introduced " in several stages in order to achieve as smooth a transition as possible ". Hence there will be further changes, but for the moment we can only concern ourselves with the General and Particular ones which have received approval.

A. GENERAL CHANGES

(i) *Simplification of the rites*

Underlying all the changes in the Mass is the desire on the part of the Sacred Congregation of Rites to make the Mass more simple in structure. " Parts which with the passage of time came to be duplicated, or were added with little advantage, are to be omitted. Other parts which suffered loss through accidents of history are to be restored to the vigour they had in the days of the holy Fathers." (art. 50) " The rites should be distinguished by a noble simplicity. They should be short, clear and free from useless repetitions. They should be within the people's power of comprehension, and normally should not require much explanation." (art. 34)

The Council is aiming at "the elimination of all duplication, and of unintelligible ceremonial, of Mass and the other Sacraments". This will mean that in future all repetitions of the *Introit,* the lessons, etc. will be eliminated. While this seems to be purely a matter of rubrics, it nonetheless will add to the simplicity of the Mass. The Instruction now lays down the rule that "obeisances by celebrants and ministers to the choir will be made only at the beginning and the end of sacred ceremonies; only the altar at which the liturgical ceremony takes place is to be incensed; the kissing of hands and of objects given or received is to be omitted". (no. 36)

It is clear from the Instruction that "the entire order of the Mass will have to be reformed" (no. 48), and so we can expect further changes following from the above principle. These may well include the many blessings over the Sacred Species after the Consecration. One such blessing has now been omitted, during the doxology at the end of the Canon of the Mass.

(ii) *A proper division of rôles*

The Mass is composed of several parts, some which pertain to the celebrant, others to the choir and the people. In sung Masses there will be the rôles of the deacon and subdeacon. The Instruction now states that "if the parts which belong to the choir and people are chanted or recited by them, they must not be said privately by the celebrant". (no. 32) "Similarly the celebrant must not say privately the readings which are read or sung by the competent minister or the altar-server." (no. 33) This is but an amplification of the ruling laid down in the Constitution: "In liturgical celebrations each person, minister or layman, who has an office to perform, should carry out all and only those parts which pertain to his office by the nature of the rite and the principles of the liturgy." (art. 28)

All this will mean a change in our attitude towards the various functionaries who participate in the Mass. It will mean that all who take part must do so with proper dignity and decorum. The details of the matter are outlined in the Instruction nos. 49-52.

(iii) *The Liturgy of the Word*

The Constitution in art. 51 had stated that "the treasures of the Bible are to be opened up more lavishly so that a richer fare may be provided for the faithful at the table of God's word. Thus a more representative part of the sacred scriptures will be read to the people in the course of a prescribed number of years". The Instruction now lays down the regulation that "In public Masses, the Lessons, the Epistle and the Gospel, are to be read or sung facing the people." (no. 49) We have already seen that the vernacular may be used in such readings. From this it is clear that the first part of the Mass, the liturgy of the Word, is now intended to be given more prominence. Provisions are made for the reading by the celebrant himself, or in a solemn Mass to be seated, while listening.

Here we have a return to the more authentic way of conducting the first part of the Mass. Already in a bishop's Mass some semblance of this was evident, when the bishop presided at the throne. But now ordinary priests may preside at the liturgy of the word, while the deacon, subdeacon or lector read the prescribed parts, and the choir chants.

The liturgy of the word will take place away from the altar in a solemn Mass. At a read Mass the celebrant will use an ambo or lectern, and face the people while reading. In this way the words of sacred scripture will be *directed* more clearly to the faithful.

The aim is to make this first part of the Mass more didactic in character. The early Christians borrowed this custom of reading the Bible at Mass from the synagogue worship as practised among the Jews. Our non-Catholic brethren have maintained a good tradition by providing a worthy reading of the word of God. The Catholic Church is now restoring an ancient custom to its former place of honour. It is very probable that in years to come we shall have longer and better-chosen passages from scripture read at Mass, with a more liberal use of the Old Testament. The Mass, therefore, provides the most excellent opportunity for the reading of the Word of God to the people of God.

In order to provide for the actual fulfilment of this prescription, the Instruction in no. 92 legislates that " a seat for the celebrant and ministers should be so placed that it will be clearly visible by the faithful, and that the celebrant himself will be clearly seen to be presiding over the assembly ". Likewise no. 96 states that " it is fitting to have an ambo for the sacred readings. They should be so placed that the ministers using them can be clearly seen and heard by the people ". These provisions are easy and simple and should not give any great difficulty to priests.

In future, therefore, the priest, deacon, subdeacon or lector will *face* the people while reading. In this way he can " proclaim " the Word of God, as a herald who proclaims good news. The sacred readings will have a greater impact on the listeners in this way. It is possible to point to doctrinal, pastoral and psychological reasons for a return to the older way of facing the congregation. (McManus)

(iv) *The Eucharistic liturgy*

The second part of the Mass will take place *at the altar*. In this way the Banquet-Sacrifice will stand out more clearly. The altar is both the table of the Lord's Supper and the table of the sacrifice. With the celebrant facing the people, this will be easier to grasp than in the former custom of having his back to them. The people will be able to follow more closely the sacred action, for no longer will the priest shield the Sacred Species from them.

The new rite will make the second part of the Mass less of a hidden, secret action. The priest looks up and extends his hands to say " The Lord be with you ", and thus does not seem to interrupt the ceremony, as happened when he had to turn around to address the congregation with these same words. Likewise, when he says " Brethren, pray that my sacrifice and yours may be acceptable to God the Father Almighty ", he does so without any sign of interruption. In fact, it will become more evident that the priest will feel the people to be *with him* as he performs his sacred function, while in their turn the people will feel themselves more *with the priest* at the altar.

The Mass will become the action of the whole people of God, who offer it with the priest. They will participate in the Mass in a more natural and genuine way. They give their assent to the sacrifice and they partake of the sacrament in Holy Communion. Special care should be taken to ensure that the Lord's Prayer is recited with dignity by all, and that the rich doctrine of this prayer is understood by them. Likewise the faithful should be instructed to make their act of faith in the Eucharist by answering a clear " Amen " when the priest says " Corpus Christi " at Holy Communion. Other details of changes in the Eucharistic Liturgy will be indicated in the following section. All that needs to be stressed here is the fact that the changes in the Mass have re-established a better balance in its whole structure. As a result the faithful should be able to participate in the Mass with greater devotion and understanding. It is once again evident that pastoral reasons have dictated the new reforms. It may take some time to appreciate the new pastoral values involved, but they most certainly are there, waiting to be tapped.

B. PARTICULAR CHANGES IN THE MASS

(i) *The Entrance rite*

The new form of the entrance rite is noteworthy for three reasons. First of all, it should be a *procession*. It would be ideal if the priest and ministers could walk up the centre aisle, with the acolytes carrying candles. The people should stand all this time, and only kneel when the celebrant reaches the altar.

Secondly, the *Judica me* psalm is omitted. The use of this psalm 42 with its antiphon *Introibo* dates from about A.D. 1000 (Martimort). It is absent from the Dominican rite and also from those of Milan and Lyon. In fact it only became a fixed element in the Roman liturgy with the reform of the missal by Pius V. It has always been considered as the private preparation of the celebrant for Mass; because it serves no direct pastoral purpose it has now been dropped.

Thirdly, considerable emphasis is now laid on the recitation of the *Confiteor*. There have been numerous forms of the *Confiteor* used throughout the centuries. Our present one dates from about the year 900 and was composed somewhere in the Rhineland. The words are simple and can be recited with sincerity and understanding by all. At some future date it may be possible to have the celebrant reciting the *Confiteor* with the congregation. The present doubling seems to run counter to the general principles of the new reform.

We can, indeed, consider this public confession of sins as having a quasi-sacramental character, especially as the words used by the celebrant after it: "May Almighty God have mercy on us . . ." "May the Almighty and merciful God grant us pardon, absolution and remission of our sins", are used in sacramental confession. In any case, the recitation of the *Confiteor* satisfies the basic need to purify ourselves before offering sacrifice, and as such it serves a very worthy and excellent purpose.

The verses which follow: "Turn to us, O Lord, your mercy" are a further plea to God for forgiveness of our sins. They serve as an introduction to the prayer *Aufer a nobis,* which the priest says as he climbs the steps to the altar (Martimort). The celebrant then kisses the altar, which is a symbol of Christ. It was only in late medieval times that this kiss was considered as honouring the saints whose relics were kept in the altar stone. The multiplication of kisses during the Mass is also a medieval growth. In the earliest times it was only when he approached the altar for the first time and when he finally left it that the celebrant kissed the altar, and the action was meant to symbolise a salute and a farewell to Christ, whom the altar represented.

The *Kyrie, Gloria* and Collect(s) belong to the Entrance rite, but as they will be studied in a later section (The People's Part in the Mass), there is no need to elaborate on them here. The only point worth mentioning is that the celebrant should pause for a few seconds after saying "Oremus" before beginning the Collect. The "Oremus" is addressed to the congregation, whereas the actual Collect is addressed to God. ("Let us pray . . . O God . . .") This rule should apply to all prayers preceded by "Oremus".

(ii) *The Liturgy of the Word*

There is a clear contrast and difference between the Entrance rite and the Liturgy of the Word. The former is all movement, singing, common prayer. In the latter, the congregation are either seated or standing, in an attitude of listening and attention. While the Entrance rite is basically a *preparation*, with its confession of guilt, pleas for mercy, etc., the Liturgy of the Word is a *celebration*—in its own right—of the living Word of God. In this part of the Mass the faithful are nourished spiritually and mentally. The sacred readings are meant to be understood by them, so that the seed of the Word of God may bear abundant fruit in their souls.

The Word of God is read *in the assembly*. It is not a private reading, but a public act of the Church. There must be a certain solemnity about the reading and proclaiming of the Epistle and Gospel; it is a test of the faith of both reader and listeners. It is at this stage that the People of God are first confronted with the Mystery of God, speaking to them in human language, but presenting them with His message, which is now offered for their spiritual nourishment. It is here that we realise the importance of making a deeper study of the Bible, and acquainting ourselves as far as possible with both Old and New Testaments.

The Constitution has declared that " the treasures of the Bible are to be opened up more lavishly so that a richer fare may be provided for the faithful at the table of God's word ". (art. 51) We should note the word " treasures ". The Bible is a treasure-house of spiritual food for our souls. Those who know how to use the Bible properly can lay hold of immense wealth. And it is above all in the Mass that this spiritual wealth is held out to us.

As has already been said, the Liturgy of the Word takes place *away from the altar*. The celebrant or the reader faces the congregation, and he reads in a language understood by them. In giving such prominence to this part of the Mass, the Council Fathers have wished to restore it to its former place of honour. All should be present for these sacred readings. The Word of God is always active and it calls for a response. Hence the faithful will not receive it passively, but will feel themselves involved, by eating "at the table of God's word".

(iii) *The Homily*

Some of us will be put off by this word "homily". It seems to recall much too vividly some of the drier lessons or homilies of the Fathers which we read in our breviaries. The Constitution has decided on the word "homily" because it is traditionally the word used for an explanation of the Word of God. Having read the Word of God to the assembly, the celebrant now breaks this spiritual bread for them. The homily is one particular form of sermon, most suited to the purpose and end outlined by the Constitution.

"The 'homily from the sacred text' is to be understood to be either an explanation of certain aspects of the readings from Sacred Scripture, or of some other text from the Ordinary or the Proper of the day, taking into account, however, the mystery which is being celebrated and the peculiar needs of the congregation". (art. 54) The homily is, therefore, always related to the Mass. The word "homily" is from the Greek, and means "to accompany" or "to go together". And in this case it is meant to accompany the Sacred readings, to follow immediately upon the Gospel. It is not a catechetical instruction or a meditation on a pious subject; it is a continuation of the Word of God, a part of the heralding of the Good News.

There are two reasons why the homily should be restored to its original place of honour. First of all, the Word of God must be *explained* to the People of God, and it must be explained within the context of certain Sunday celebrations or feasts. The homily is an essential " link " between the Mystery of the Mass and the mystery being celebrated this particular Sunday or feast day. The Homily makes present this mystery and allows the faithful to contemplate it with some measure of understanding. It is a " breaking of the Word of God " to suit the needs of this particular congregation. And in order to bring out more clearly the connection between the sacred reading and the homily, both should be delivered from the same area (sanctuary or ambo). It would be a definite break in this continuity if the celebrant were to make his way to the pulpit for the homily.

Secondly, the Word of God must be made *to live* in the hearts of the faithful. Hence the celebrant must not limit himself to mere explanations of the sacred text; he must arouse the faith of his congregation and help them to see how they are involved in the Word of God. For it is the *living* Word of God that is now being preached, and in opening up the secrets of the divine message the preacher must not be satisfied with mere generalisations. He must come down to the level of his people, who are hungry for the Word of God. The Word of God can and should effect a change in their lives, give them something to live for, make them realise that there is another life beyond the grave, and that the mysteries of our religion are all links in a tremendous chain which binds us all to God.

All the commentators have stressed the importance of the homily in the new reform of the Mass. One of them goes so far as to say that " the overall result of the reform of the liturgy promulgated by the Constitution will depend in great measure on the way this prescription of the Constitution is carried out ". (Jounel) That it will call for much effort on the part of the clergy there is no doubt, but the results will be of immense spiritual benefit to their flocks.

(iv) *The Prayer of the Faithful*

The Constitution has laid it down that "the 'common prayer' or 'prayer of the faithful' is to be restored after the gospel and homily, especially on Sundays and holydays of obligation. By this prayer in which the people are to take part, intercession will be made for holy Church, for the civil authorities, for those oppressed by various needs, for all mankind, and for the salvation of the entire world". (art. 53) The Instruction states that "the celebrant is to direct the prayer from the celebrant's seat, or from the altar, the ambo or the altar-rails". (no. 56)

It is the wish of the Council Fathers that this ancient form of prayer be restored to the Mass. At the present moment, the only time this "prayer of the faithful" appears in our public worship is on Good Friday, in the so-called Bidding Prayers. It has often been noticed how the priest says "oremus" just before the Offertory antiphon; but in fact the *Oremus* always introduces a prayer, not an antiphon. This "Oremus" originally introduced the prayer of the faithful. It was so-called, because it was the first time at the Mass when the celebrant addressed "the faithful" alone. Up to then the catechumens had been present in the church. This prayer or litany was offered by the faithful for all the needs of the Church and of mankind. It was a universal and truly Catholic prayer. There were many varieties of form used, and the Council has not imposed any set formula. It will be left to the competent ecclesiastical authorities in different countries to draw up their own prayer of the faithful. It is to be noted that the Constitution foresees that this prayer will be said in the vernacular (art. 54) and that the congregation will join in. It is most probable that the form to be used will be more simple than that of the Good Friday liturgy, which has nine actual prayers.

Fr. Reinhold has adapted and translated one such prayer used in Germany, which goes like this:

Cel.: Let us pray. Lord Jesus Christ, Son of the living God, obedient to the will of the Father unto death on the cross.
All: Have mercy on us.
Cel.: For our holy Father Pope Paul, our bishops and priests, let us pray.
All: Lord have mercy on them.
Cel.: For our government and all who serve us in public office, let us pray.
All: Lord have mercy on them.
etc.

It is a very simple form of prayer, and will serve to bring the people of God more into the picture at this part of the Mass. It will serve also to indicate that the Mass is not a private action, but rather that it is the greatest public service mankind can perform here on earth. The prayer of the faithful will be a community prayer, said in the form of a dialogue, and will unite all the separate worshipping groups of Christians throughout the world. It will serve as a bond between ourselves and the Oriental rites, and also with the Protestant liturgies which have preserved the " bidding prayers ". (McManus)

(v) *The Orate Fratres and the Secret*

Now that the *Orate Fratres* is to be said in the vernacular, it will be necessary to explain its meaning to the people. Originally it was addressed by the celebrant to the clergy who stood around the altar, but later on it was extended to include the whole congregation. In some cases the celebrant said "Pray, brothers *and sisters*. . . ."(Jungmann) The Orate Fratres is a petition for prayer which retains a personal character: "that *my* sacrifice and *yours* ". In the earliest ordinals there was no set response. This petition for prayer occurs at that part of the Mass when the presentation and preparation of the gifts is completed.

The reply which the people make is a very beautiful and meaningful one: "May the Lord receive the sacrifice from your hands, to the praise and glory of His name, for our benefit and that of all His holy Church ". Again we notice the *personal* theme. It is meant to be said slowly and deliberately and with understanding. The priest has offered the bread and wine in the name of the congregation and of the whole Church. The people now make this offering of their own accord and with clear intent. Hence the reply to the Orate Fratres is no empty formula, but is rather a rich and convinced statement made by all present whereby they unite themselves with the priest at this moment of the Mass.

The Instruction now directs that the Secret(s) be said or chanted aloud. The so-called Secret-prayer was originally a prayer over the offerings, said aloud at the end of the offertory-rite. It was a prayer *over* the bread and wine. (*Oratio super oblata*). In the eighth century in northern France we find the first evidence of this prayer being said silently (Jungmann), in keeping with the Gallo-Frankish custom of praying silently as often as possible.

(vi) *The doxology at the end of the Canon.*

The Instruction directs that the doxology is to be chanted or said aloud; during the whole of the doxology the celebrant is to hold the chalice and the host slightly elevated; he is to omit the signs of the cross and, at the end, he is to genuflect only after the people have answered " Amen ". (no. 48f)

Here we have something new, although in fact it is only a return to a more ancient and authentic custom. We note that the actual words of the doxology are in the indicative form (*est*), instead of the subjunctive or wishing form. The words which accompany the rite indicate or point out that it is *through* Christ, and *with* Him and *in* Him that all honour and glory are given to the Father. Hence the rite is meant to focus attention upon the Sacred Species, and this is done in fact by the little elevation. The making of the five crosses, which formed part of the rite up to this, is of late medieval origin (c. 1000). All kinds of symbolic reasons were given for the five crosses, v.g. they represented the five wounds. But in the ancient Roman custom these crosses were not " an exercise of the power of blessing but rather a strengthening and stylising of the demonstrative or pointing gesture which is inherent in the elevation itself ". (Jungmann) And this was the only elevation of the Mass at the time.

The new regulation, omitting the crosses at the doxology, is of tremendous significance. It means that the multiplication of such gestures as the sign of the cross is now considered as unnecessary, and we can expect further reduction in them. All this will lead to a noble simplicity, which is one of the aims of the present reform of the Mass.

The doxology brings the Canon to a close. It is Trinitarian in form, and is richer and more ornate than other doxologies. It is meant as a means of arousing the faithful to make a great act of faith in the sacrifice of the Mass, and hence their assent was expected with an enthusiastic cry of " Amen ". This " Amen " was considered as having more significance than those given to other prayers in the Mass, and it is to be hoped that our congregations will rise to the occasion when the reform is introduced.

(vii) *No Last Gospel or Leonine prayers.*

The omission of the Last Gospel comes as no surprise. The first historical evidence we have of the use of the prologue of the Gospel of St. John at this part of the Mass is in the middle of the 13th century. It was first used by the Dominicans but was not generally regarded as part of the Mass. As it was recited silently, it served no pastoral purpose. In fact it had become something of an " anticlimax " (Reinhold) to the Mass. It seemed to put the blessing and dismissal into wrong focus. Fr. Jungmann declared that there was something " incongruous, something discordant about this last point of the Mass-liturgy. This is shown by the fact that there is no actual proclamation of the Gospel, no public reading of it ".

The Mass now ends with the last blessing, which is the traditional way of bringing it to a close.

The omission of the Leonine prayers likewise is something which was to be expected. These prayers were introduced by Pope Leo XIII on 6 January 1884, during the Kulturkampf. Later they were designated as being for the conversion of Russia by both Popes Pius XI and XII. By their very origin they were of a temporary nature and were never intended to be a permanent part of the Mass. They were always considered as something " added " to the Mass. Following on the principle laid down in art. 50 of the Constitution, they are henceforth to be omitted.

CHAPTER VIII

PARTS WHICH BELONG TO THE PEOPLE

Already in the Instruction of the Sacred Congregation of Rites of 3 September, 1958 on Sacred Music and Liturgy, provision had been made for the external participation of the faithful at Mass: "The participation of those present is, however, more complete, if external participation is added to internal attention, that is participation shown by external actions, such as bodily posture (kneeling, standing, sitting), or by ritual gestures, and especially by the responses, prayers and song". (art. 22b)

This same Instruction then went on to specify the ways in which this could be done, and the following is the ordinance laid down for "dialogue Mass":

"Finally, there is the third, the more complete, way when the faithful liturgically make answer to the celebrating priest, in a kind of 'dialogue' with him, *by reciting aloud the parts* proper to them. Four degrees of this fuller participation can be distinguished:

(a) The first degree, if the people make the easier liturgical response to the celebrant, namely: *Amen; Et cum spiritu tuo; Deo gratias; Gloria tibi, Domine; Laus tibi, Christe; Habemus ad Dominum; Dignum et justum est; Sed libera nos a malo.*

(b) The second degree, if the faithful also say the responses which, according to the rubrics, are to be recited by the server; and, if Holy Comunion is distributed within the Mass, say also the Confession and the triple *Domine, non sum dignus.*

(c) The third degree, if the people recite aloud, in

addition, with the celebrant parts of the Ordinary of Mass, namely: *Gloria in excelsis Deo; Credo; Sanctus; Benedictus; Agnus Dei.*

(d) The fourth degree, if the faithful say also with the celebrant parts from the Proper of the Mass: Introit, Gradual, Offertory and Communion." (art. 31)

The lists of those parts which pertain to the people are outlined in (a), (b) and (c). Those parts given in (d) belong to the *choir,* a section of the people, who must be specially trained. This concept of the *choir* or *schola* is something new, for they are now recognised as a section of the assembly.

In the above divisions of the parts of the Mass there is one notable exception: "The Pater Noster". The Instruction makes provision for this in art. 32: "In low Masses the *Pater Noster,* being a suitable and traditional prayer for Communion, may be recited by the faithful with the celebrating priest, but only in Latin, all adding *Amen.* Its recital in the vulgar tongue is barred". The Instruction of 26 Sept., 1964, goes further and allows the *Pater Noster* in the vernacular, (art. 57c) following upon the principles laid down in art. 54 of the Constitution: "A suitable place may be found for the vernacular in Masses which are celebrated with the people, especially in the readings and 'the common prayer', and also, as local conditions may warrant, *in those parts which pertain to the people.*"

It is now admitted by all liturgical scholars that there are certain parts of the Mass which actually belong to the faithful and which they have a right and duty to fulfil. And this part cannot be taken by a proxy, such as a server. It is only when these parts are said by all the congregation that they take on their real and complete meaning. The people must act along with and through the priest, by praying, singing, sacrificing and eating. The new reform will not bear any fruit unless we all learn to take our part in the Mass. And this will call for learning the words " by heart ", and making sure that they come " from the heart ". We must enter fully into our rôle at Mass, and participate both *externally* (by words, gestures, etc.) and *internally* (by a conscious assent to and appreciation of the acts we perform). Most of the prayers which belong to the people are short and simple, and can easily be understood by all. Hence we cannot excuse ourselves on the grounds of not being intelligent.

(i) *The Confiteor*

This common confession of guilt by the congregation is but an admission of their being creatures of flesh and blood, who stand in need of divine forgiveness and help. Although the celebrant makes his own confession, the people have their own particular occasion to confess their sins. We must see here the bond which unites all members of the Church, the same bondage of guilt and need of redemption. It is the whole Church which prays in this particular congregation; it is the people of God who stand before His altar, asking for mercy. The whole gamut of human sin is now brought before God, and will be washed away in the Blood of the Lamb.

Although in our hearts we confess our personal sins, this public act of confession at Mass is no private matter. Each one brings his own sins and puts them into the crucible, where they will join the sins of our brethren. The reciting of the *Confiteor* should be an act of *humility*. It is also a plea for God's grace, to purify us and make us worthy to enter into the divine presence. At Mass we will be meeting Our Lord, and this sacred encounter will call for proper dispositions on our part. We do not dare to enter into communication with, or into the presence of

God without proper preparation and without taking thought of our creaturehood. That is exactly what we supply by our humble and common confession of guilt.

(ii) *Lord, have mercy*

This part of the Mass, which is usually in Greek, (*Kyrie eleison* . . .) is all that remains of what was formerly a long litany. The priest suggested certain intentions for which the people should pray, and in their reponses they said " Lord, have Mercy ". We still have these same responses in the Litanies of Our Lady (of Loreto), of the Sacred Heart, etc. when we say " Lord, have mercy on us ", " Pray for us ". Whereas in the *Confiteor* we had confessed our sins, now we make a direct plea for divine mercy, and we do this to Christ, our Saviour.

The words " Lord, have mercy on us " are very ancient, and have always been the people's response. Although the words " on us " are not included, the plea is for mercy for the congregation present and for the whole Church of God. The Kyrie is of Greek origin, and did not get to Rome earlier than the fifth century. (Jungmann) The *Christe eleison* (Christ, have mercy) is of Roman origin. All nine invocations are directed to Christ. The arrangement based on these corresponds to a primitive sacral usage, which was taken over by the Church and canonised by her in her liturgy.

Originally in a sung Mass, the celebrant took no part in the *Kyrie*. It was not until the 13th century, when the priest was obliged to read the variable texts from the missal, that the celebrant began to say the *Kyrie* with his assistants. All this is evidence that it was not part of the celebrant's rôle to say the *Kyrie*. We see, therefore, that it is a prayer belonging to the people and which belongs to them in their own right.

(iii) "*Glory to God in the highest*"

This is an old Church song that has been sung in the Christian East since the fourth century as a morning hymn. (B. Fischer) It was later on adapted by the Western liturgy and made into the people's hymn as Mass. The opening words are those used by St. Luke in chapter two of his Gospel. The Church, therefore, has taken the words of the angels of Bethlehem and put them into the mouths of the people of God.

The actual hymn only begins with the words "We praise thee" and as the hymn develops it becomes something of a triumphant song. It is the hymn of the redeemed, in thanksgiving to God the Father and His Son, Jesus Christ, for having saved mankind from the evil effects of sin. There are, in fact, two parts to the hymn, the first directed to God the Father and the second to Jesus Christ. In this hymn we have a double *motif:* words of praise to God, and pleas for divine mercy for men. It is above all a *prayer,* sent from the heart, to the throne of God, a prayer which is sure to be heard. The hymn takes on its full meaning when sung on Holy Thursday or on Christmas Night, with a solemn pealing of bells and playing of the organ. But it is always the people's prayer, the people's hymn of joy and praise.

(iv) "*And also with you*"

This simple and short reply of the people to the priest's greeting "The Lord be with you", is repeated many times during the Mass. It would be a pity if we allowed it to remain an empty phrase on our lips. The words which the priest addresses to us all are very ancient and have even passed into the Irish language for everyday use: "Dia dhuit". It is a truly Christian form of greeting, corresponding to our " Good morning " or " Hello ". The usual reply to these latter forms of greeting is to repeat the same phrase by way of answer. And the same holds for the Christian greeting. The reply to " The Lord be with you " is simply " And also with you ".

In ordinary social life the man who refuses to return a friendly greeting is considered impolite. Furthermore when a reply is given there are many tones of voice which can indicate the enthusiasm or sincerity of our words. Feelings and moods enter into our normal everyday life, but they should not be allowed to influence our spiritual life. Our reply to the priest is no mere exercise of politeness, but of faith. And the depth of our faith will be the measure of our sincerity.

(v) " *Amen.*"

However short the people's response to the priest's greeting may be, there is another phrase shorter still which is constantly on their lips at Mass. The word " Amen " means " so it is " or " so let it be ". It is the giving of our assent to the words and actions of the priest. It is no mere nodding of the head in a half-hearted and grudging assent, but a full-voiced and meaningful agreement with all that the priest has said and done.

When the priest is concluding the Collect, which he says in our name, he gives us an opportunity at the end of putting our signature to his words. In this way we make his words our own, and the prayer rises to God from priest and people. Unless we give our actual assent we are not with the priest, but are on our own. This simple word " Amen " (so let it be) is an indication that we are participating, taking our rightful part in the Mass. It means that we no longer adopt the attitude of those who wish to leave everything to the priest, while they look on. The Mass is not a play or a spectacle, but a sacred action, in which we must take our part. And we do this by using such simple words as " Amen ".

When the priest comes to the end of the Canon, before he begins the " Our Father ", he asks us to give our assent to all that has been happening at the altar during the Great Prayer (i.e. the Canon). This particular " Amen " should be said with more enthusiasm than any other "Amen" in the Mass, because it is our way of putting our seal to the most solemn part of the Mass. This " Amen " has nothing to do with the " Our Father "; it is not an introduction to the Lord's Prayer, but rather the end of The Great Prayer of the Canon of the Mass. The " Amen " can never be a beginning of anything, but is always a conclusion; or rather is is a verbal assent to some sacred word or action.

We say " Amen " before we receive Holy Communion. The priest holds up the Host and says " Corpus Christi " (The Body of Christ), and we reply " Amen " (So it is). We make a clear act of Faith in the real Presence at this moment. And it is worth noting that those who are receiving Holy Communion should not close their eyes at this instant, but should look at the Host just as the priest does before he receives the Host. We make an act of Faith in the real Presence, in the Person of Christ present in the host. A clear and firm " Amen " will indicate the measure of our faith and our enthusiasm to receive Our Lord and Saviour.

(vi) " *I believe in One God* "

In the Nicene Creed we have a profession of faith, which at first glance seems to have very little to do with the Mass. Yet it does fulfil a very specific and necessary purpose. In the early days of the Church, especially during the periods of persecution, the Christians took it as a matter of honour to be able to profess their faith publicly. They were often called upon to deny Christ before the pagan judges, and to offer sacrifices to the pagan gods. As a counter-action to all this, they became more rooted than ever in the need to make their own profession of faith before the real altar of the Lord, in the Christian assembly. They felt that their faith received a definite boost by being proclaimed publicly at Mass, and the singing or recitation of the Creed was a weekly reminder to them of all their responsibilities.

It is also possible that the Creed at Mass was meant to be a renewal of our baptismal promises. It was introduced into the Mass as a community act, as "the avowal of the whole believing congregation. Necessarily, then, it ought to be spoken (or sung) by the whole congregation". (Jungmann) It is said standing, and should be a joyful proclamation of our faith.

The Creed follows the Gospel, and the homily. It was inserted at this point of the Mass because it served as a follow-up to the proclamation and explanation of the Word of God. It is a kind of "re-enforced echo" (Jungmann) of the Gospel message. While our actual text of the Creed was not composed for reciting at Mass, it has now become an accepted part of it on Sundays and feast days.

It is quite clear that the Creed is no private prayer. It it not sufficient for the priest to say it for us, we must make it our own by saying (or singing) it along with him. It is a community act, one of our means of participating in the Mass. In reciting the Creed our minds should reflect on the truths which it proclaims. It is a solemn profession of our faith in Jesus Christ, in the remission of sin, in the resurrection of the body and life everlasting. In this way it serves to prepare our minds for a worthy offering of the sacrifice of the Mass and the reception of the Sacrament of the Lord's Body.

(vii) *Responses before the Preface*

At the beginning of the Canon of the Mass the priest addresses the people, and enters into a dialogue with them. "Lift up your hearts," "We have lifted them up to the Lord." The words of the priests are almost like a command, a signal, a tocsin. And the people reply that they are ready, their hearts are raised to the Lord. This is one of the most ancient formulas in the Church's liturgy; it takes the place of the "Let us pray" before the Great Prayer. Although there is a certain solemnity about the words used, they are in fact simple expressions of Christian faith and hope.

When we admit to having our hearts raised to the Lord, we must feel it our duty to turn our back on earthly matters. Our thoughts cannot always be on God, but at this most solemn moment of the Mass we now make a communal effort to raise our minds and hearts to Him. This raising of our hearts to God is a fundamental attitude of Christian prayer. And as the Great Prayer (i.e. the Canon) of the Mass begins, we associate ourselves with the priest, so that all present unite themselves with him in one great act of worship.

We should, therefore, say these words with devotion and attention, and they should be an expression of a fact, i.e. that we have our minds directed towards God. However distracted we may have been at Mass up to this point, we should now bring our wandering minds back to contemplating God. There will be no need to ring a bell to warn us that the Canon of the Mass is now about to begin. We should be fully awake and alive to what is happening and about to happen at the altar. Thus united with the priest in offering sacrifice, our minds are turned to the Lord, and we are disposed properly to fulfil our rôle at Mass.

In the next part of the dialogue the priest says: "Let us give thanks to the Lord our God," to which we reply: "It is right and proper." The important word is that used by the priest "thanks", for our reply only reiterates his words by saying that "It is right and proper to give thanks". There are many reasons why a Christian should give thanks, and this public acclamation of thankfulness is most appropriate at Mass. The Mass is itself a great act of thanksgiving to God for having redeemed us.

The words used by the congregation are full of spiritual depth and meaning. While each one can give thanks for the blessings of God which have come to him, yet it is above all as a community that we make this solemn declaration of thanksgiving. Priest and people together give thanks, in the name of the whole Church. Thus our cry is the cry of all the people of God, and we associate ourselves with the great thanksgiving prayer of the Mass which is about to begin.

(viii) *The Sanctus-Benedictus*

The Sanctus is a continuation of the Preface, but whereas the latter was said or sung by the celebrant, the former is said or sung by the whole congregation. The *Sanctus* is a victory *hymn,* and hence it is meant to be sung. Having lifted our hearts to God, we are now raised on high, and join our voices with those of the angels in heaven. The Constitution reminds us of this in art. 8: "In the earthly liturgy we take part in a foretaste of that heavenly liturgy which is celebrated in the Holy City of Jerusalem towards which we journey as pilgrims . . . With all the warriors of the heavenly army we sing a hymn of the Lord's glory . . ."

The Victory Hymn consists of the two lines:

"Holy, holy, holy, Lord God of Hosts!
Heaven and earth are full of Thy Glory!"

and originally this was all that followed the Preface. This hymn in honour of God's holiness is an echo of the first phrase of the Lord's Prayer: "Hallowed be thy name." We should notice the combination of the two words in the hymn "heaven *and* earth". According to the Jewish tradition the Presence of God was limited to the Temple; but in Christian tradition God has now pitched His tent among men. It is Christ who has joined heaven and earth together, by His victory over sin, death and the devil. Our hymn is an expression of joy at Christ's victory, which we now share in.

While the *Sanctus* is taken from the Old Testament (Isaiah and Daniel), the *Benedictus* is a New Testament motif, as is also the line "Hosanna in the highest!" The *Sanctus* is a hymn of adoration, whereas the *Benedictus* is a hymn of praise. One is addressed to God the Father, the other to God the Son. Both add up to a perfect triumphant hymn, which recalls the scene of Christ's entry into Jerusalem on the first Palm Sunday. We now greet Christ, Who will come upon our altar in a few moments.

(ix) *The Our Father*

The *Our Father* introduces what we may call "The Communion Cycle" of the Mass; it is the first of a series of prayers and actions which are directed towards the partaking of the sacrifice in Holy Communion. There is evidence of this prayer in the West since the fourth century, although its present position was arranged by Pope Gregory the Great. It is introduced by " Oremus " (Let *us* pray) and it is clearly meant to be said or sung by all present. The *Our Father* is essentially a community prayer, and traditionally has been closely associated with the Communion.

The Fathers of the Church repeatedly interpret the phrase in the *Our Father*: " Give us this day our daily bread " as referring to Holy Communion. In the Communion Service for Good Friday, as soon as the deacon has brought the Blessed Sacrament to the altar, the celebrant and all the congregation say aloud the Our Father. There is no doubt that this prayer has always been associated with, and used as a preparation for Communion. In fact it would not be going too far to say that it has become a meal prayer, a grace. (B. Fischer) The sacrificial gift on the altar is now to become our sacrificial food. This is our daily bread, and it is presumed that all who are present at Mass will eat of it. Art. 32 of the 1958 Instruction calls the *Our Father* " a traditional prayer for Communion ".

There is another phrase in the *Our Father* which is appropriate at this moment of the Mass: " Forgive us our trespasses ", in which we ask for the forgiveness of our sins. This is a final purification, a final act of humble admission of our creaturehood, as we prepare ourselves to approach the table of the Lord. It was the custom of the clergy in St. Augustine's town of Hippo, to strike their breasts as they pronounced these words.

(x) *The Agnus Dei*

We may well wonder how the *Agnus Dei* should be considered as belonging to the people's part of the Mass. There is no doubt about the fact that it is of Eastern origin; it was customary there to refer to the sacrificial gifts as the "Lamb". The phrase "Lamb of God" is taken from St. John's Apocalypse, and refers to the sacramental Christ when used in the Mass. Hence the priest, when holding up the Host before distributing Communion to the faithful says: "Behold *the Lamb of God.*"

In the seventh century we have evidence of the use of the *Agnus Dei* in Rome, as a chant to accompany the fraction of the bread. Originally, therefore, it had some connection with the breaking of the Bread at the altar, which the priests did in imitation of Christ, who at the Last Supper, broke bread. For nearly a thousand years the Church used ordinary leavened bread, which was brought by the people in the form of loaves and placed upon the altar at the Offertory. The priest broke them into small pieces before Holy Communion, and this ceremony of breaking the Bread often took a long time. In order to fill in the time the people chanted the *Agnus Dei*. The priest was completely occupied with his task of breaking the Bread, and it is very unlikely that he said it at all. (Jungmann) The *Agnus Dei* belonged to the people, it was their final act of greeting Christ before receiving Him in Holy Communion.

The *Agnus Dei* was familiar to the people, as it formed part of the litanies, and the words "Lamb of God, Who takest away the sins of the world, have mercy on us", were repeated as often as was necessary, until the priest had completed breaking the Bread. It was only when the Church turned over to using unleavened bread, and the practice of breaking the loaves had been abandoned, that the litany was shortened and reduced to a triple invocation of the Lamb.

Our attitude during the singing or reciting of the *Agnus Dei* should be that of waiting for Holy Communion, making our final preparation for It. It is a prayer of adoration, and we should bow our heads slightly. The triple invocation is directed towards Christ in the Eucharist, Christ Who is the Paschal Lamb. The Constitution on the Sacred Liturgy reminds us that the Mass is "a paschal banquet in which Christ is consumed". (art. 47) As we all recite the *Agnus Dei* we turn our minds towards Our Saviour, Who laid down His life for us, and Who offered Himself as a spotless Victim to the Father. We beg Him to grant us mercy and peace, two things which He alone can give.

(xi) *"Lord, I am not worthy . . ."*

The use of the Centurion's phrase from the Gospel: "Lord, I am not worthy that thou shouldst enter under my roof, say but the word and my son shall be healed," with the change of only one word "son" to "soul", has accompanied the Communion rite since the tenth century. Although the phrase is said in the singular "*my* roof", "*my* soul" it is ideally suited for use by all at this moment of receiving Holy Communion. Even though we are a community worshipping together, we are also individuals, with responsibility for our own souls. We come to Mass to offer it as a pleasing sacrifice to the Father, Who in return gives us His Son in Holy Communion.

And, indeed, we need Christ, for He is the great Physician of our souls. He alone can "heal" us, He alone can wipe away our sins. Thus, while Holy Communion is Food for our souls, it also serves to heal our sickness and make us spiritually strong. The words which we use: "Lord, I am not worthy . . ." while they imply a deep reverence, also include a note of confidence. As we recite them we should look towards the Host which the priest holds in his hand, and make a last humble act of faith and humility.

(xii) *Deo Gratias* (Thanks be to God)

At the very end of Mass, the priest, just before giving us his final blessing, utters the official words of dismissal.

In Roman times it was customary at every official or public meeting to have someone announce the end of the meeting. They had a sense of order, and no one would have thought of leaving the assembly without the official word of dismissal being given. In their turn, the people replied " good " or " thanks ". But the Christians wished to make their reply more sacred, and thus while imitating the normal Roman procedure of dismissal, they give it a Christian turn. Hence their " thanks " to the person who dismissed them, became " Thanks be to God ".

We are expected, therefore, to make an effort to say these words with conviction. In this way we show that we have been participating in the Mass, and we are glad that we have been able to do so. We remember, too, that the Mass is a thanksgiving and that we Christians will never have finished saying " Thanks " to God for His many gifts. We thus leave the church with these words on our lips, and show our appreciation of the Mass.

PART III

THE RESULTS

CHAPTER IX

A GREATER SPIRITUAL ENRICHMENT

Obviously the Council Fathers have not decided to change the Mass in its external form, without at the same time achieving something at the internal level. It is clear that what the reform aims at above all else is the deepening of our understanding of the Mass. In other words, we are now expected to see the Mass in a new light, to view it with a greater spiritual maturity.

The very process of growth and change leads normally to maturity. Life itself is always on the move. Activity, not passivity, is the law of super-nature as well as of nature. No human being can stand still, be a static personality. In like manner, the Mass was never meant to be an unchanging entity, for it had to be re-examined every so often in the light of changing circumstances, changing cultures. Those who advocate that the Mass should be "freezed", left alone, unchanged, show themselves to be out of touch with reality and life itself. The Mass has not got to change in its essential elements, in those parts which are of divine institution, but the human elements can and ought to be changed from time to time. (art. 21) These human elements have to change to suit us; it is because we have changed that the Mass must do likewise.

This spiritual enrichment is to be achieved on two levels: that of *the community* of the people of God, and on *the individual* level. Over the centuries we have allowed some of our fundamental rights to be exercised by proxy. The altar boy has taken our rightful place at the altar. In fact we had reached the stage where, as a community, we had ceased to exercise our rightful duties and functions. Now that the Council has reminded us of our rightful part in the Mass, we, as a community, must respond with enthusiasm.

This will call for a greater sense of being a community as we stand before the altar of the Lord at Mass. Instead of being an incoherent, divided group of worshippers, we now come to church as a mature Christian community. We ought to think of the days in ancient Rome when the Christians met to celebrate Mass. It was, to a certain extent, a *closed* community, but no one can deny that they were mature. They often had to give evidence of their maturity by shedding their blood. The days of martyrdom have gone; we no longer run any risks in being Christians; we are never put to the test. Our sense of being a community is limited, because we do not feel the need of the community's protection.

But the reforms of the Mass will lead to such a community spirit that we shall all feel united and one. As we pray and sing, stand and sit together, we will feel bound to each other and part of a community. And as we become more proficient in our united efforts, then will our sense of community mature and bear fruit. The new reform of the Mass will bring a great re-awakening of community fervour. It may be slow in coming, but that is the aim we should set ourselves.

All this will not mean that we have to change fundamentally ourselves. The result will come from the impact of the liturgy upon us as a community. Provided that we take our part, play our rôle, it will, slowly but surely, forge us into a mature Christian community. There is a lot of work to be done in the Church before this final goal is reached. But priests and people must be filled with a holy enthusiasm for the changes which the Council Fathers have introduced.

We can also hope for a spiritual enrichment *at the individual level.* Each one of us will ask himself the question: "Why am I being asked to change my ideas, my way of offering Mass?" And there is only one answer: "You are being offered new signposts to help guide your personal life to its ultimate goal." That is what the Church is doing in her reform of the Mass: she is putting up new signposts so that we can make our way more clearly, so that we can travel along the road with greater ease.

There will be, of course, some who will see in the reforms of the Mass some kind of obstruction in their way. They have got so used to the old road, that they are afraid of meeting unexpected obstacles on the new one. Perhaps they will even go so far as to see the reforms as so many sets of traffic lights, controlling every mile of the road, and they will imagine that the lights are always turned to Red. Such an attitude is not a mature one. The reforms are only signposts, clearly indicating the way we should go. They will not obstruct, but rather will help us along, provided we make the effort to read them properly.

Let us remind ourselves once again of the words of Pope John to the Fathers of the Vatican Council, when he spoke of the "new Pentecost" which was being achieved in the Church today. The Spirit which came upon the Apostles and disciples of Our Lord that first Pentecost morning is still with us. And just as He worked a mighty change in each of those who sat in the upper-room in Jerusalem so He has the power to change each one of us. It would be almost like resisting the Spirit to refuse to be moved to better things.

Yet we remain responsible for our own individual selves. No one can force us to adopt or accept the new reform. At least no one can force us to adopt them with *a willing heart* and *an open mind.* But the success of the reform among Catholics will depend upon the individual efforts to keep an open mind and to have a willing heart each time we come to Mass. We may feel out of things at first, we may feel strangers, we may be distracted and ill at ease. All these things are part of our maturing process. Gradually we will come to see the value of the changes which have been introduced. We will then be able to take our rightful part in the Mass, and be proud to fulfil our rôle in an adult and mature way.

Much will depend too upon which generation we belong to. The older generation will find it more difficult to adjust itself to new ways. But they owe it by way of example to the younger generation to put their heart and soul into the new reform. The Church has reached a cross-roads, and she is anxious to gather all her children into one mighty group. She is anxious about the future of her children, and the reforms have been introduced as a means of keeping her children close to her. And we keep close to her by falling into line with her liturgical reforms.

This spiritual maturity will enrich our lives more than we can imagine. It will no longer be a question of *attending* Mass, but of offering it and taking a full part in it. By the fact of our Baptism we have been given a share in Christ's priesthood. The seed of divine life then planted in our souls is meant to grow, to mature. It is by exercising our rights as fully-fledged and adult Christians that we prove we have reached maturity. We must not be led to think that it is only in heaven that we shall be able to please God and exercise our spiritual faculties. Already here on earth, through the liturgy, we can do this. It is our privilege as the people of God, as members of the Church, to take an active part in celebrating the liturgy of the Mass.

This spiritual maturity will show itself in our being committed to give ourselves completely to God and to our neighbour. We must not hold ourselves back when dealing with God. He has given us everything, and He expects our everything in return. It is, above all, at Mass that we learn to give, for the Mass is the greatest act of self-giving which we can experience here on earth. It is the re-enactment of Christ's self-giving to the Father, and as such is the perfect sacrifice.

We will also learn to appreciate the timelessness of the Mass, for the Mass is for all time, not just for this or that period or era. The Mass is our great link with Christ, with the Last Supper, the Passion and Death, the Resurrection and Ascension. The Mass links us with the early Christians in Jerusalem, with the martyrs in Rome and elsewhere, with the past generations of Christians, who have handed down to us this precious heritage. It is an historical link between all Christians of all times, the great unifying element. And each generation and age must make the Mass their own.

That is what the Constitution wishes to achieve, to make the Mass part of the second-half of the 20th century. It must integrate itself upon modern man, bear its own stamp, but also bear the stamp of our day. One of the obvious results of the reform will be this realisation among Christians of their responsibility of keeping the Mass "alive". It will call for some adaptation, but it will leave us all the richer in the end.

While the reform of the Mass is very much the concern of the bishops and clergy, the Constitution insists that the laity be in the picture, too. The laity have an important part to play in the missionary work of the Church. The Mass will fill the faithful with a zeal for the spread of God's kingdom on earth. The Constitution puts it this way: "The renewal in the Eucharist of the covenant between the Lord and man draws the faithful into the compelling love of Christ and sets them on fire . . . Christ's faithful, though not of this world, are to be the lights of the world and are to glorify the Father before men." (arts. 10, 9) This is an invitation, a call to the lay apostolate, pointing out the Mass as the source of all spiritual strength and energy. Having learned to take an active part in the Mass, we will be led to take an active part in the missionary work of the Church. This will not mean that we must set out for foreign lands. Every country is a missionary country in one sense of the word. There are always " others " who need our prayers and charitable help, and charity should begin at home!

CHAPTER X

THE PASCHAL MYSTERY IN THE CHRISTIAN LIFE

Anyone who has kept abreast of recent theological development will be aware of the new approach to the study of the sacraments. The sacraments are now viewed in their biblical and liturgical dimensions, and as such are seen to be the pivot and centre of the Christian life. The Constitution on the Sacred Liturgy, while it is disciplinary, is also *doctrinal* in intent. Its aim is to give the Mass and the other sacraments greater meaning in our lives.

> " The purpose of the sacraments is to sanctify men, to build up the body of Christ, and, finally, to give worship to God. Because they are *signs* they also instruct. They not only presuppose faith, but by words and objects they also strengthen and express it . . . It is, therefore, of the greatest importance that the faithful should frequent with the greatest eagerness those sacraments which were instituted to nourish the Christian life." (arts. 59 and 60)

The key word in the above passage is " sign ". A sign is an aid to knowledge, a means of identifying things, a means of communication with others. When the policeman on traffic duty raises his hand, motorists know that this is a sign for them to stop. When we are lost along some country road and we come across a signpost, this will indicate to us the way we want to go. A sign loses its value if it cannot be easily understood. A sign is an external thing or action, indicating some material fact or message.

Now while the sacraments are signs, they are special kinds of signs, *sacred signs*. They are sacred actions, having three aims in view: "to sanctify men, to build up the body of Christ, and to give worship to God." (art. 59) They are also meant *to instruct*, and the faithful should be able to understand the signs easily. There should be no need for numerous explanations. (Cf. art. 34)

It is one of the aims of the Constitution to make "the intimate connection between rite and words more apparent in the liturgy". (art. 35) Here we have something new: the faithful should be *easily* able to understand the sacred signs. "Pius X had introduced the idea of *active participation;* Pius XII had indicated that this participation should be *conscious;* now the Second Vatican Council introduces a third factor: *easy*." (Roguet) The aim of the reform of the Mass is to allow the faithful to participate *actively, consciously* and *easily* in the Church's public worship. For the Mass is a sacred action, an external rite, demanding our assent and approval as well as our participation and appreciation.

We see, therefore, that the Constitution has an immediate Pastoral aim in view: to make the Mass more easily understood by the faithful, and to allow them to join fully in it. (art. 21) St. Augustine often remarked how Christian worship was contrasted with pagan rites by its very simplicity. The Mass was a less complicated ceremony in St. Augustine's day than ours. Hence the Constitution is anxious to restore this simplicity to our Mass. Certain symbolical actions, which have lost their meaning for modern man, will be omitted, and other rites, difficult of explanation, will be dropped. An example of this is the former practice of the sub-deacon at High Mass holding the Paten from the Offertory to the *Pater*, with the Humeral Veil around his shoulders. (Instruction, no. 48d)

The important thing is that the rite should be a sign of

a sacred nature, which should lead the faithful to understand its meaning, and which should be a means of nourishing their devotion and piety. They should not be lost in trying to grasp the separate actions, but should be able to see the Mass as a whole. And it is in this context that we come to see why the Constitution places such importance on the Paschal Mystery.

The Instruction sums this up in one key passage:

> "Pastoral activity which is centred on the liturgy aims to make the Paschal Mystery be expressed in men's lives. It was in the Paschal Mystery that the Son of God incarnate, having been obedient unto the death of the cross, was raised so high by His resurrection and ascension that He was able to share His own divine life with the world, in such wise that men who had been dead in sin and were now made like to Christ 'may not now live to themselves, but unto Him who died for them, and rose again.'" (no. 6)

The Mass brings us into contact with the Paschal Mystery, and enables it to overflow into our lives. But what do we mean by the Paschal Mystery? Is it just a theological expression? The Constitution would have us take a close look at the words:

"The wonderful works of God among the people of the Old Testament were but a prelude to the work of Christ Our Lord in redeeming mankind and giving perfect glory to God. He achieved his task principally *by the Paschal Mystery of his blessed passion, resurrection from the dead, and glorious ascension.*" (art. 5)

The Paschal Mystery is seen as working itself out at three levels. First of all, God had prepared His Chosen People by bringing them from the captivity of Egypt, and guiding them across the Passage of the Red Sea. The Hebrews passed over from slavery and death, to freedom and life.

And they celebrated God's wonderful deliverance by eating annually of the paschal lamb, a rite ordained by God Himself.

Secondly, when the fullness of time had come, Christ became Man, and by His passion, death, resurrection and glorification achieved a greater victory and a greater deliverance than had been given to the Jews of old. He offered Himself as a victim for the sins of the world, and became our Paschal Lamb. He passed over to the Father from this world, through offering Himself as a sacrifice for sin. And just when He was about to offer Himself, He shared His last supper with His disciples. It was at this moment that He instituted the Eucharist, and gave His apostles the power to offer It in memory of Him. " Do this for a commemoration of me." At this moment he established the new covenant of His Love, which was to overflow into the lives of all men. *The* Paschal Mystery is that which surrounds the Passion, Death, Resurrection and Ascension of Christ.

Thirdly, the Church, true to Christ's command, now celebrates in her liturgy the Paschal Mystery. In this way she makes present once again the redeeming work of Christ. It is not only during Holy Week that the Church does this, but at every Mass. From the first Pentecost Day until the end of time the Mass will be the Church's great act of commemorating Christ's redeeming sacrifice. " From that time onwards the Church has never failed to come together to celebrate the Pascal Mystery." (Constitution, art. 6)

But the Paschal Mystery is meant to overflow into our lives; it is meant to be the source of our Christian life: " The liturgy, in its turn, moves the faithful filled with ' the paschal sacraments ' to be ' one in holiness '; it prays that ' they hold fast in their lives to what they have grasped by their faith '." (art. 10) Now it is in the very act of taking our full part in the Mass that we lay hold of, and enter into, the Paschal Mystery. Christ did not die and rise for Himself, but *for all men*. And God does nothing in vain. What He does must have results. However, we are men, with free will, and God requires our free co-operation with Him. Hence it follows that each one of us must give himself freely and consciously to the work of making the Paschal Mystery overflow into his own life.

Underlying all the separate parts of the Mass, we must see it as bringing us into contact with the Paschal Mystery. The first part of the Mass: the Liturgy of the Word, will feed our minds with heavenly knowledge, and bring us into contact with Christ in the scriptures. All the readings will relate in some way or other to Christ. The doctrinal content of Epistle and Gospel, and their explanation in the Homily, will prepare our minds to celebrate the Paschal Mystery. But the Liturgy of the Word doesn't simply set the stage, as it were. It brings us Christ Himself, making Him present in His word, and our minds are nourished at the table of the Lord's word. We contemplate the Paschal Mystery as related for us in the sacred readings, and seek to apply this great mystery to our own lives.

The second part of the Mass, the Liturgy of the Eucharist, is directed primarily towards celebrating the Paschal Mystery. It is the Church, acting on the orders of Christ, which now offers once again a perfect Sacrifice to the Father. It is the whole Church that accomplishes this great Act. And it is as members of the Church that we can join in the sacrifice. By virtue of our Baptism we are privileged to share in offering the Mass, through the hands of the priest, and to share in the eating of the Body of Our Lord.

If we could only penetrate into the depths of the mystery of the Mass we would appreciate the Council's urgent cry to all Christians to participate more fully in it. The Mass *must* and *should* change our lives. The Mass is the centre of our faith, the source of endless graces. It communicates to us the mystery of salvation. It is the great Sign, indicating the fact of the redemption. The Constitution on the Sacred Liturgy wishes that this Sign become more easily recognised by Christians for what it is, the greatest gift of God to men.

What the Council wishes is that Christians try to live the Paschal Mystery themselves, in and through the liturgy. Although the Church celebrates the mystery of Christ in Holy Week and Easter and re-enacts then the full pageant of the Paschal Mystery in her solemn celebrations, there is a paschal element in all her feasts, and also in her Sunday Masses. And this paschal character is meant ultimately to overflow into our lives.

The Constitution makes it quite clear that we have at hand all the opportunities and means for doing this, and enumerates them as follows: Baptism, renunciation of sin, Penance, the Eucharist, prayer and personal mortification. (art. 6) This is a vast programme, but its aim is to make us Christ-like, to have us imitate Christ. It is not just a question of a past event becoming real to us, of bringing back an historical fact and making it present once again. It is the Person of Christ that serves as the link, because Christ is eternally present as our High-Priest, yesterday, today and tomorrow. In the liturgy we once again meet Christ, and it is *in* Him, and *through* Him that we get the power to become other Christs.

The power of Christ comes to us in the Mass and the other sacraments, in our personal contact with Him in prayer, and by our sacrifices and charity. It is the mystery of the risen Christ taking hold of us, and working upon us, transforming us into His image.

It is possible to go one stage further in our understanding of the Mass in this context of the Paschal Mystery. The Mass is a sacred action, and this sacred action or *sign* leads not to any place or thing, but to a Person. Although Christ died and rose from the dead, and now reigns in heaven, His Presence among us is made possible by means of the Mass and the other sacraments. It is above all in the Mass that we *encounter* Christ. Every time we participate in celebrating Mass we join in a communal act of meeting Christ.

The Mass is, therefore, the great meeting-point between Christ and His Church. The whole intention of the Mass ritual is to make His Presence real for us: the Bread and Wine become the Body and Blood of Christ. By receiving Christ in Holy Communion we enter into personal contact and union with Him. The Mass is the great act of thanksgiving, which the Church will never tire of making, and we offer this thanksgiving in the Presence of Our Saviour. The Parish Sunday Mass is the weekly and communal meeting with Christ to thank Him for the Redemption.

The Mass makes present once again the Paschal Mystery. We offer to the Father the Spotless Lamb, Who has taken away the sins of the world. We pledge ourselves to serve God and to love Him, and in this way the Mass overflows into our daily lives. As the Constitution says: "The liturgy 'through which the work of our redemption is accomplished', most of all in the divine Sacrifice of the Eucharist, is the outstanding means whereby the faithful may express in their lives and manifest to others the mystery of Christ and the real nature of the true Church." (art. 2)

CHAPTER XI

VATICAN II, THE MASS AND THE CHURCH

At the beginning of this book we saw how Pope John set out to achieve an "aggiornamento" in the Church. Vatican II was to be the instrument whereby this renewal of Christian life and the bringing of the Church up to date would be effected. The four points or aims of the Vatican Council have been stated; they have yet to be made a reality. And it is clear that the Mass will play a considerable rôle in making real the Council's proposals.

But it is interesting, by way of conclusion, to see what the Council's latest document: the Constitution "De Ecclesia" (On the Church)[1] has to say on the Mass. For it is the Mass *in* the Church, and celebrated *by* the Church which is the main-spring of the Christian life. The Constitution on the Sacred Liturgy is completed by that on the Church. Only some of the key-passages will be chosen, and they will help us to link together some of the ideas which have already been considered in earlier chapters.

First of all, the Church is called "the dwelling-place of God", "the House of God", "the temple". (art. 6) Now, the Mass is celebrated in the dwelling-place of God, in His temple. The very name we give to our place of worship, *church,* indicates how holy a place it is, and what holy symbolism it is surrounded with. Every time we enter the church for Mass, we enter into our true home, into our

---

[1] All quotations from the Constitution De Ecclesia have been taken from the unofficial translation, published in *The New York Times* (International ed.), 24 Nov. 1964.

new city. Our places of worship are sacred places, for they are images of the new Jerusalem. We should have a deep reverence for our churches, not only because they are the places where we offer the Sacrifice of the Mass, but because they are an image of heaven.

Secondly, the Constitution of the Church reminds us that the Mass brings us into union with Christ and with each other: "Really partaking of the body of the Lord in the breaking of the eucharistic bread, we are taken up into communion with Him and with one another . . . In this way all of us are made members of His body". We are reminded that "the life of Christ is poured into the believers who, through the sacraments, are united in a hidden and real way to Christ who suffered and was glorified." (art. 7)

Thirdly, the dignity of all baptised Christians is stressed, as giving them the right to share fully in the Sacrifice of the Mass. "The baptised, by regeneration and the anointing of the Holy Spirit, are consecrated as a spiritual house and a holy priesthood, in order that through all those works which are those of the Christian man *they offer spiritual sacrifices* and proclaim the power of Him who has called them out of darkness into His marvellous light . . . *The faithful, in virtue of their royal priesthood, join in the offering of the eucharist.* They likewise exercise that priesthood in receiving the sacraments, in prayer and thanksgiving, in the witness of a holy life, and by self-denial and active charity." All this is but a re-echo of the words of the Constitution on the sacred Liturgy (cf. arts. 6 and 12)

Fourthly, the organic structure of the Church is underlined, and we see ourselves as all belonging to the same Community: "It is through the sacraments and the exercise of the virtues that the sacred nature and organic structure of the priestly community is brought into operation. Incorporated in the church through baptism, the faithful are consecrated by the baptismal character to the worship of the Christian religion". (art. 11) What the Council is telling us here is that by our baptism we not only *ought to* participate fully in the liturgical life of the Church, but that we are not fully-Christian unless we actually *do* participate to the full. There is no cause for dissension among the people of God, or for division among the various members. The Mass is to be the unifying element, which will bring all together, in one common bond, united in and through the Sacrifice of Our Lord.

Finally, the Mass is seen to overflow beyond the needs of the Christian community out into the world, for " All men are called to belong to the new people of God". " The Catholic Church strives constantly and with due effect to bring all humanity and all its possessions back to its source in Christ . . ." This is something really vital, and something which we must understand. Christ came to save *all men.* We Christians are called to share in Christ's work of saving the world. Our religion is not an exclusive one, but opens its doors to all. For all men are brothers. As the Constitution on the Church puts it: " Those who have not yet received the Gospel are related in various ways to the people of God . . . The Church both prays and labours in order that the entire world may become the people of God, the body of the Lord . . ." (art. 17)

The Church thus strikes a universal note and sends out an appeal to her children to co-operate in saving the world. This is to be done chiefly by prayer and sacrifice. It is to be achieved on the community level by offering the Mass for the spread of the faith, and on the individual level, by our personal prayer and sacrifice. The Council sees this work done by all the members of the Church. The laity have their part to play: " Even when preoccupied with temporal cares, the laity can and must perform a work of great value for the evangelisation of the world". (art. 35)

Here we have the whole basis of the " aggiornamento " which Pope John desired with all his heart. For we bring the world with us when we come to worship God. We can consecrate not only ourselves, but the whole world, to God at Mass. The Constitution on the Church gives us this final assurance:—

> " For all the works, prayers, apostolic endeavours of the laity, their ordinary married and family life, their daily occupations, their physical and mental relaxations, if carried out in the spirit, and even the hardships of life, if patiently borne—all these become spiritual sacrifices acceptable to God, through Jesus Christ. Together with the offering of the Lord's body, they are most fittingly offered in the celebration of the eucharist. Thus . . . the laity consecrate the world itself to God." (art. 33)

Thus we see that the Council has set us a tremendous programme. The changes which have been introduced into the Mass are only made to allow us to fulfil our rôles in the Church more fruitfully and worthily. Praise, honour and glory are given to God through the Church's worship, while graces are given to men by God at the same time. We have to associate ourselves with this *upward* and *downward* movement of intercourse between heaven and earth. The Council has issued a challenge to all Christians, and the Church awaits their response.

A SHORT READING LIST

A SHORT READING LIST

Ephermerides Liturgicae, Vol. 78 (1964) fasc. III-IV.

Doctrine and Life, Feb., 1964.

The Furrow, May and Nov., 1964.

La Maison-Dieu (1964), nos. 76 and 77.

Worship, Vol. 38 (1964), nos. 7, 8 and 9.

J. D. Crichton, *The Church's Worship.* Chapman. 1964.

Austin Flannery, ed. *Vatican II: The Liturgy Constitution.* 3rd ed. Scepter. 1964.

The Assisi Papers. Proceedings of the First International Congress of Pastoral Liturgy. The Liturgical Press. Collegeville. 1957.

Pope Pius XII: *Christian Worship.* The Encyclical Letter *Mediator Dei.* C.T.S. London. 1954.

The Sacred Congregation of Rites. Instruction on Sacred Music and Liturgy, issued 3 Sept., 1958. ed. J. B. O'Connell. Burns & Oates. 1959.

B. Fischer, *God's People about the Altar.* The Liturgical Press. Collegeville. 1961.

Hovda, ed. *Sunday Morning Crisis.* Helicon. 1964.

C. Howell, *Your Part in the Mass,* London. L. J. Cary. 1964. (A pamphlet.)

J. A. Jungmann, *The Mass of the Roman Rite.* Its origins and developments. One-volume edition of *Missarum Sollemnia.* Burns & Oates. 1959.

A. Kirchgaessner, *Unto the Altar.* Herder-Nelson. 1962.

C. Korolevsky, *Living Languages in Catholic Worship.* Longmans. 1957.

J. Léon-Dufour, Duplacy and others: *Vocabulaire de theologie biblique*. Ed. du Cerf. 1962.

A. G. Martimort ed. *L'Eglise en Prière*. Introduction à la liturgie. Desclee. 1961.

A. G. Martimort, *The Signs of the New Covenant*. The Liturgical Press. Collegeville. 1963.

S. C. Lennon, *English in the Mass*. Australian C.T.S. pamphlet. Melbourne. 1964.

J. B. O'Connell, *Active Sharing in Public Worship*. Burns & Oates. 1964.

J. Richard Quinn, *God's People at Mass*. Benziger. 1964.

H. A. Reinhold, *Bringing the Mass to the People*. Burns & Oates. 1960.

L. Shepherd, *Blueprint for Worship*. Longmans, Darton & Todd. 1964.

Studies in Pastoral Liturgy. Vol. I ed. Placid Murray, O.S.B. Vol. II ed. Vincent Ryan, O.S.B. Furrow-Gill. 1961, 1963.

D. R. Ward, *The Mass is Yours*. London C.T.S. pamphlet. 1964.

What is the Liturgical Movement? by the Priests of St. Severin and St. Joseph. Faith & Fact Book. Burns & Oates. 1964.

APPENDICES

APPENDIX I

THE CONSTITUTION ON THE SACRED LITURGY

CHAPTER I

GENERAL PRINCIPLES FOR THE RESTORATION AND PROMOTION OF THE SACRED LITURGY

1°. *The Nature of the Sacred Liturgy and its importance in the life of the Church.*

5°. God who "wills that all men be saved and come to the knowledge of the truth" (I Tim. 2:4) "who in many times and various ways spoke of old to the fathers through the prophets" (Hebr. 1:1), when the fullness of time had come sent his Son, the Word made flesh, anointed by the Holy Spirit, to preach the gospel to the poor, to heal the contrite of heart,[1] to be a bodily and spiritual medicine,[2]: the Mediator between God and man.[3] For his humanity united with the Person of the Word was the instrument of our salvation. Therefore, "in Christ the perfect achievement of our reconciliation came forth and the fullness of divine worship was given to us".[4]

The wonderful works of God among the people of the Old Testament were but a prelude to the work of Christ Our Lord in redeeming mankind and giving perfect glory to God. He achieved his task principally by the paschal mystery of his blessed passion, resurrection from the dead, and glorious ascension, whereby "dying, he destroyed our death, and rising, restored our life".[5] For it was from the side of Christ as he slept the sleep of death upon the cross that there came forth "the wondrous sacrament of the whole Church".[6]

---

[1] Cf. Is. 61:1; Luke 4:18.
[2] St. Ignatius of Antioch, *Ad Ephesios*, 7:2.
[3] Cf. 1 Tim. 2:5.
[4] *Sacramentarium Veronese* (Leonianium).
[5] Easter Preface of the Roman Missal.
[6] Prayer before Second Lesson of Holy Saturday (Roman Missal, before restoration).

6°. Accordingly, just as Christ was sent by the Father so also he sent the apostles, filled with the Holy Spirit. This he did so that they might not only preach the gospel to every creature[7] and proclaim that the Son of God by his death and resurrection had freed us from the power of Satan[8] and from death, and brought us into the Kingdom of his Father, but also that they might carry into effect the work of salvation they preached by means of the Sacrifice and sacraments around which the entire liturgical life revolves. Thus by *Baptism* men are grafted into the paschal mystery of Christ; they die with him, are buried with him, and rise with him,[9] they receive the spirit of adoption as sons "in which we cry, Abba, Father" (Rom. 8:15), and thus become true adorers such as the Father seeks.[10] In like manner as often as they eat the *Supper of the Lord* they proclaim the death of the Lord until he comes.[11] Wherefore, on the very day of Pentecost when the Church appeared before the world those "who received the word." of Peter "were baptised". And "they continued steadfastly in the teaching of the apostles and in the communion of the breaking of bread and in prayers . . . praising God and being in favour with all the people" (Acts 2:41-47). From that time onwards the Church has never failed to come together to celebrate the paschal mystery, reading those things "which were in all the scriptures concerning him" (Luke 24:27), celebrating the Eucharist in which "the victory and triumph of his death are again made present",[12] and at the same time "giving thanks to God for his unspeakable gift" (2 Cor. 9:15) in Christ Jesus, "in praise of his glory" (Eph. 1:12) through the power of the Holy Spirit.

7°. To accomplish so great a work Christ is always present in his Church, especially in her liturgical celebrations. He is present in the Sacrifice of the Mass not only in the person of his minister, "the same now offering, through the ministry of priests, who formerly offered himself on the cross",[13] but especially in the eucharistic species. By his power he is present in the sacraments so that when anybody baptises it is really Christ

---

[7] Cf. Mark 16:15.
[8] Cf. Acts 26:18.
[9] Cf. Rom. 6:4; Eph. 2:6; Coloss. 3:1; Tim. 2:11.
[10] Cf. John 4:23.
[11] Cf. 1 Cor. 2:26.
[12] Council of Trent, Session 23: Decree on the Holy Eucharist, c. 5.
[13] Council of Trent, Session 22: Doctrine on the Holy Sacrifice of the Mass, c. 2.

himself who baptises.[14] He is present in his word since it is he himself who speaks when the holy scriptures are read in the church. Lastly, he is present when the church prays and sings, for he has promised "Where two or three are gathered together in my name there am I in the midst of them" (Matt. 18:20).

Christ, indeed, always associates the Church with himself in this great work wherein God is perfectly glorified and men are sanctified. The Church is his beloved bride who calls to her Lord, and through him offers worship to the eternal Father.

Rightly, then, the liturgy is regarded as an exercise of the priestly office of Jesus Christ. In the liturgy the sanctification of man is signified by signs perceptible to the senses, and is effected in a way which corresponds to each of these signs. In the liturgy the whole public worship is performed by the Mystical Body of Jesus Christ, that is, by the Head and his members.

From this it follows that every liturgical celebration, because it is an action of Christ the Priest and of his Body, which is the Church, is a sacred action surpassing all others. No other action of the Church can equal its efficacy by the same title and to the same degree.

8°. In the earthly liturgy we take part in a foretaste of that heavenly liturgy which is celebrated in the Holy City of Jerusalem towards which we journey as pilgrims, where Christ is sitting at the right hand of God, Minister of the holy things and of the true tabernacle.[15] With all the warriors of the heavenly army we sing a hymn of the Lord's glory; venerating the memory of the saints, we hope for some part and fellowship with them; we eagerly await the Saviour, Our Lord Jesus Christ, until he our life shall appear and we also will appear with him in glory.[16]

9°. The sacred liturgy does not exhaust the entire activity of the Church. Before men can come to the liturgy they must be called to faith and to conversion. "How then are they to call upon him in whom they have not believed? And how are they to believe in him whom they have not heard? And how are they to hear without a preacher? And how are men to preach unless they be sent?" (Rom. 10:14-15).

Therefore the Church announces the good tidings of salvation to those who do not believe, so that all men may know the one

---

[14] Cf. St. Augustine, *Tractatus in Ioannem VI*, c. 1, note 7.
[15] Cf. Apoc. 21:2; Coloss. 3:1; Hebr. 8:2.
[16] Cf. Philipp. 3:20; Coloss. 3:4.

true God and Jesus Christ whom he has sent and may be converted from their ways, doing penance.[17] To believers also the Church must ever preach faith and penance; she must prepare them for the sacraments, teach them to observe all that Christ has commanded,[18] and invite them to all the works of charity, piety and the apostolate. For all these works make it clear that Christ's faithful, though not of this world, are to be the lights of the world and are to glorify the Father before men.

10°. Nevertheless the liturgy is the summit towards which the activity of the Church is directed. At the same time it is the fount from which all her power flows. For the object of apostolic works is that all who are made sons of God by faith and baptism should come together to praise God in the midst of his Church, to take part in the Sacrifice and to eat the Lord's Supper.

The liturgy, in its turn, moves the faithful filled with "the paschal sacraments" to be "one in holiness"[19]; it prays that "they hold fast in their lives to what they have grasped by their faith".[20] The renewal in the Eucharist of the covenant between the Lord and man draws the faithful into the compelling love of Christ and sets them on fire. From the liturgy, therefore, and especially from the Eucharist, grace is poured forth upon us from a fountain, and the sanctification of men in Christ and the glorification of God to which all other activities of the Church are directed, as towards their end, are achieved in the most efficacious way possible.

11°. But in order that the liturgy may be able to produce its full effects it is necessary that the faithful come to it with proper dispositions, that their minds should be attuned to their voices, and that they should co-operate with heavenly grace lest they receive it in vain.[21] Pastors of souls must, therefore, realise that, when the liturgy is celebrated, something more is required than the laws governing valid and lawful celebration. It is their duty also to ensure that the faithful take part fully aware of what they are doing, actively engaged in the rite and enriched by it.

12°. The spiritual life, however, is not limited solely to participation in the liturgy. The Christian is indeed called to pray

---

[17] Cf. John 17:3; Luke 24:27; Acts 2:38.
[18] Cf. Matt. 28:20.
[19] Postcommunion for both Masses of Easter Sunday.
[20] Collect for Mass on Tuesday of Easter Week.
[21] Cf. 2 Cor. 6:1.

with others, but he must also enter into his bedroom to pray to his Father in secret;[22] furthermore, according to the teaching of the apostle, he must pray without ceasing.[23] We also learn from the same apostle that we must always carry around in our body the dying of Jesus, so that the life also of Jesus may be made manifest in our mortal flesh.[24] That is why we beg the Lord in the Sacrifice of the Mass that "receiving the offering of the Spiritual Victim" he may fashion us for himself "as an eternal gift".[25]

13°. Popular devotions of the Christian people, provided they conform to the laws and norms of the Church, are to be highly recommended, especially where they are ordered by the Apostolic See.

Devotions proper to individual churches also have a special dignity if they are undertaken by order of the bishops according to customs or books lawfully approved.

But such devotions should be so drawn up that they harmonise with the liturgical seasons, accord with the sacred liturgy, are in some way derived from it and lead the people to it, since in fact the liturgy by its very nature is far superior to any of them.

II.—LITURGICAL INSTRUCTION AND ACTIVE PARTICIPATION

14°. Mother Church earnestly desires that all the faithful should be led to that full, conscious and active participation in liturgical celebrations which is demanded by the very nature of the liturgy, and to which the Christian people "a chosen race, a royal priesthood, a holy nation, a redeemed people" (I Peter 2:9, 4-5) have a right and obligation by reason of their baptism.

In the restoration and promotion of the sacred liturgy the full and active participation by all the people is the aim to be considered before all else, for it is the primary and indispensable source from which the faithful are to derive the true Christian spirit. Therefore, pastors of souls must earnestly strive to achieve it in all their pastoral work.

Yet it would be futile to entertain any hope of realising this unless pastors of souls, in the first place, themselves become fully imbued with the spirit and power of the liturgy and become

---

[22] Cf. Matt. 6:6.
[23] Cf. 1 Thess. 5:17.
[24] Cf. 2 Cor. 4:10-11.
[25] Secret for Monday of Pentecost Week.

thoroughly masters of it. Thus it is absolutely essential, first of all, that steps be taken to ensure the liturgical training of the clergy. For that reason the Sacred Council has decided on the following enactments:

15°. Professors who are appointed to teach liturgy in seminaries, religious houses of studies and theological faculties, must be properly trained for their work in institutes which specialise in this subject.

16°. The study of sacred liturgy is to be ranked among the compulsory and major courses in seminaries and religious houses of studies. In theological faculties it is to rank among the principal courses. It is to be taught under its theological, historical, spiritual, pastoral and juridical aspects. In addition, professors of other subjects shall take care, especially those who teach dogmatic theology, sacred scripture, spiritual and pastoral theology, that while striving to expound the mystery of Christ and the history of salvation from the angle proper to each of their subjects, they nevertheless clearly set forth the connection between their subject and the liturgy, and the unity which underlies all priestly training.

17°. In seminaries and houses of religious clerics shall be given a liturgical formation in their religious life. For this they will need proper direction so that they may be able to understand the sacred rites and participate in them wholeheartedly, both in the celebration of the sacred mysteries as well as in other popular devotions which are imbued with the spirit of the sacred liturgy. Likewise they must learn to observe the liturgical laws so that life in seminaries and religious institutes may be thoroughly influenced by the liturgical spirit.

18°. Priests, both secular and religious, who are already working in the Lord's vineyard are to be helped by every suitable means to a fuller understanding of what they do when they perform sacred rites, to live the liturgical life and to share it with the faithful entrusted to their care.

19°. With zeal and patience pastors of souls must promote the liturgical instruction of the faithful and also their active participation, both internal and external, taking into account their age, condition, way of life and standard of religious culture. By so doing pastors will be fulfilling one of the chief duties of a faithful dispenser of the mysteries of God, and in this matter they must lead their flock not only by word but also by example.

20°. Transmission of the sacred rites by radio and television, especially in the case of Mass, shall be done with discretion and dignity, under the leadership and direction of a suitable person appointed by the bishops for that office.

THE REFORM OF THE SACRED LITURGY

21°. In order that the Christian people may more certainly derive an abundance of graces from the sacred liturgy, holy Mother Church desires to undertake with great care a general restoration of the liturgy itself. For the liturgy is made up of unchangeable elements divinely instituted, and of elements subject to change. These latter not only may be changed but ought to be changed with the passage of time, if they have suffered from the intrusion of anything out of harmony with the inner nature of the liturgy or have become unsuited to it. In this restoration both texts and rites should be drawn up so as to express more clearly the holy things which they signify. The Christian people, as far as is possible, should be able to understand them with ease and take part in them fully, actively, and as is proper to a community.

Wherefore, the Sacred Council establishes the following general norms:

A: GENERAL NORMS

22°. §1. Regulation of the Sacred Liturgy depends solely on the authority of the Church, that is, on the Apostolic See, and, as laws may determine, on the bishops.

§2. In virtue of power conceded by law, the regulation of the liturgy within certain defined limits belongs also to various kinds of competent territorial bodies of bishops which have been legitimately established.

§3. Therefore no other person, even if he be a priest, may add, remove or change anything in the liturgy on his own authority.

23°. In order that sound tradition be retained, and yet the way remain open to legitimate progress, a careful investigation, based on theological, historical and pastoral grounds, should always be made into each part of the liturgy which is to be revised. Furthermore the general laws governing the structure and meaning of the liturgy must be studied in conjunction with the experience derived from recent liturgical reforms and from the indults to various places.

Finally, there must be no innovations unless the good of the Church genuinely and certainly requires them, and care must be taken that any new forms adopted should in some way grow organically from forms already existing.

Care must be taken, as far as possible, to avoid notable differences between the rites used in adjacent regions.

24°. Sacred scripture is of the greatest importance in the celebration of the liturgy. For it is from it that lessons are read and explained in the homily, and psalms are sung. The prayers, collects and liturgical hymns are scriptural in their inspiration, and it is from the scripture that actions and signs derive their meaning. Hence in order to achieve the restoration, progress and adaptation of the sacred liturgy it is essential to promote the warm and living love for sacred scripture, to which the venerable tradition of Eastern and Western rites gives testimony.

25°. The liturgical books are to be revised as soon as possible. Experts are to be employed on this task, and bishops from various parts of the world are to be consulted.

B: NORMS DRAWN FROM THE HIERARCHIC AND COMMUNAL NATURE OF THE LITURGY

26°. Liturgical services are not private functions but are celebrations of the Church which is "the sacrament of unity", namely, "the holy people united and arranged under their bishops".[26]

Therefore, liturgical services pertain to the whole Body of the Church. They manifest it, and have effects upon it. They affect individual members (of the Church) in different ways, according to their differing rank, office and actual participation.

27°. Whenever rites, according to their specific nature, make provision for communal celebration involving the presence and active participation of the faithful, it is to be stressed that in so far as it is possible this method of celebrating them is to be preferred to a celebration that is individual and quasi-private.

This applies with special force to the celebration of Mass (even though every Mass has of itself a public and social nature) and to the administration of the sacraments.

28°. In liturgical celebrations each person, minister or layman,

---

[26] St. Cyprian "On the Unity of the Catholic Church", 7; cf. Letter 66, n. 8, 3.

who has an office to perform, should carry out all and only those parts which pertain to his office by the nature of the rite and the principles of the liturgy.

29°. Servers, readers, commentators and members of the choir also exercise a genuine liturgical function. They ought, therefore, to discharge their office with the sincere piety and decorum demanded by so exalted a service and which the people of God rightly expect of them.

Consequently they must all be deeply imbued with the spirit of the liturgy, each in his own measure, and they must be trained to perform their functions in a correct and orderly manner.

30°. To promote active participation the people should be encouraged to take part by means of acclamations, responses, psalms, antiphons, hymns, as well as by actions, gestures and bodily attitudes. And at the proper time a reverent silence should be observed.

31°. The revision of the liturgical books must carefully make provision of rubrics also for the people's parts.

32². In the liturgy, apart from the distinction arising from liturgical function or sacred orders and the honours due to civil authorities in accordance with liturgical laws, no special exception is to be made for any private persons or classes of persons whether in the ceremonies or by external display.

C: NORMS BASED ON THE DIDACTIC AND PASTORAL NATURE OF THE LITURGY

33°. Although the sacred liturgy is principally the worship of the divine majesty it likewise contains much instruction for the faithful.[27] For in the liturgy God speaks to his people, and Christ is still proclaiming his gospel. And the people reply to God both by song and prayer.

Moreover the prayers addressed to God by the priest who, in the person of Christ, presides over the assembly, are said in the name of the entire holy people and of all present. And the visible signs which the sacred liturgy uses to signify invisible divine things have been chosen by Christ or by the Church. Thus not only when things are read "which were written for our instruction" (Rom. 15:4), but also when the Church prays or sings or

---

[27] Cf. Council of Trent, Session 22: "On the Holy Sacrifice of the Mass", c. 8.

acts, the faith of those taking part is nourished, and their minds are raised to God so that they may offer him their reasonable service and more abundantly receive his grace.

Wherefore in the revision of the liturgy the following general norms should be observed.

34°. The rites should be distinguished by a noble simplicity. They should be short, clear and free from useless repetitions. They should be within the people's power of comprehension, and normally should not require much explanation.

35°. That the intimate connection between rite and words may be apparent in the liturgy:

(1) In sacred celebration a fuller, more varied and more suitable reading from sacred scripture should be restored.

(2) Because the sermon is part of the liturgical action the most suitable place should be indicated even in the rubrics as as far as the nature of the rite allows. The ministry of preaching is to be fulfilled with the utmost faithfulness and exactitude. The sermon, moreover, should draw its content mainly from scriptural and liturgical sources, as proclaiming God's wonderful works in the history of salvation, or from the mystery of Christ ever made present and operative in us, especially in the celebration of the liturgy.

(3) Instruction which is more explicitly liturgical should also be given in a variety of ways. If necessary, short directives to be spoken by the priest or proper minister should be provided within the rites themselves. But they should occur only at the more suitable moments and should be in prescribed or similar words.

(4) Bible services should be encouraged, especially on the vigils of the more solemn feasts, or some weekdays of Advent and Lent, and on Sundays and Holydays, especially in places where no priest is available. In this case a deacon or some other person authorised by the bishop should preside over the celebration.

36°. §1. The use of the Latin language, with due respect to particular law, is to be preserved in the Latin rites.

§2. But since the use of the vernacular whether in the Mass, the administration of the sacraments or in other parts of the liturgy, may frequently be of great advantage to the people, a wider use may be made of it, especially in readings and directives, in some prayers and chants according to the regulations laid down separately in subsequent chapters.

§3. These norms being observed, it is for the competent territorial ecclesiastical authority mentioned in Article 22 §2, to decide whether, and to what extent, the vernacular language is to be used. Also, where circumstances warrant it, this authority is to consult with bishops of neighbouring regions which have the same language. Their decrees have to be approved or confirmed by the Apostolic See.

§4. Translations from the Latin text into the vernacular for use in the liturgy must be approved by the competent territorial ecclesiastical authority already mentioned.

E: PROMOTION OF THE LITURGICAL LIFE IN DIOCESE AND PARISH

41°. The bishop is to be considered as the High Priest of his flock from whom the life in Christ of his faithful is in some way derived and upon whom it in some way depends.

Therefore all should hold in the greatest esteem the liturgical life of the diocese centred around the bishop, especially in his cathedral church. They must be convinced that the pre-eminent manifestations of the Church consists in the full, active participation of all God's holy people in these liturgical celebrations, especially in the same Eucharist, in a single prayer, at one altar, at which the bishop presides surrounded by his college of priests and by his ministers.[28]

42°. But as it is impossible for the bishop always and everywhere to preside over the whole flock in his church he must of necessity establish groupings of the faithful; and among these the parishes, set up locally under a pastor who takes the place of the bishop, are the most important, for in some way they represent the visible Church constituted throughout the world.

Therefore the liturgical life of the parish and its relation to the bishop must be fostered in their thought and practice among the faithful and clergy. Efforts must also be made to encourage a sense of community within the parish, above all in the common celebration of the Sunday Mass.

---

[28] Cf. St. Ignatius of Antioch: Ad Magn. 7; Ad Phil. 4; Ad Smyrn. 8.

CHAPTER II

THE MOST SACRED MYSTERY OF THE EUCHARIST

47°. At the Last Supper, on the night he was betrayed, our Saviour instituted the eucharistic sacrifice of his Body and Blood. This he did in order to perpetuate the sacrifice of the Cross throughout the ages until he should come again, and so to entrust to his beloved spouse, the Church, a memorial of his death and resurrection: a sacrament of love, a sign of unity, a bond of charity,[29] a paschal banquet in which Christ is consumed, the mind is filled with grace, and a pledge of future glory is given to us.[30]

48°. The Church, therefore, earnestly desires that Christ's faithful, when present at this mystery of faith, should not be there as strangers or silent spectators. On the contrary, through a good understanding of the rites and prayers they should take part in the sacred action, conscious of what they are doing, with devotion and full collaboration. They should be instructed by God's word, and be nourished at the table of the Lord's Body. They should give thanks to God. Offering the immaculate victim, not only through the hands of the priest but also together with him, they should learn to offer themselves. Through Christ, the Mediator,[31] they should be drawn day by day into ever more perfect union with God and each other, so that finally God may be all in all.

49°. For this reason the sacred Council having in mind those Masses which are celebrated with the faithful assisting, especially on Sundays and holydays of obligation, has made the following decrees so that the sacrifice of the Mass, even in the ritual forms (of its celebration) may have full pastoral efficacy.

DECREES

50°. The rite of the Mass is to be revised in such a way that the intrinsic nature and purpose of its several parts, as well as the connection between them, may be more clearly manifested,

---

[29] Cf. St. Augustine, "Tractatus in Ioannis Evangelium", c. 6, n. 13.

[30] Roman Breviary: Feast of Corpus Christi: 2nd Vesp. Antiph. to Magnificat.

[31] Cf. St. Cyril of Alexandria: Commentary on Gospel of St. John, bk. 11, c. 11-12.

and that devout and active participation by the faithful may be more easily achieved.

For this purpose the rites are to be simplified, due care being taken to preserve their substance. Parts which with the passage of time came to be duplicated, or were added with little advantage, are to be omitted. Other parts which suffered loss through accidents of history are to be restored to the vigour they had in the days of the holy Fathers, as may seem useful or necessary.

51°. The treasures of the Bible are to be opened up more lavishly so that a richer fare may be provided for the faithful at the table of God's word. Thus a more representative part of the sacred scriptures will be read to the people in the course of a prescribed number of years.

52°. By means of the homily the mysteries of the faith and the guiding principles of the Christian life are expounded from the sacred text during the course of the liturgical year. The homily, therefore, is to be highly esteemed as part of the liturgy itself. In fact at those Masses which are celebrated on Sundays and holydays of obligation, with the people assisting, it should not be omitted except for a serious reason.

53°. The "common prayer" or "prayer of the faithful" is to be restored after the gospel and homily, especially on Sundays and holydays of obligation. By this prayer in which the people are to take part, intercession will be made for holy Church, for the civil authorities, for those oppressed by various needs, for all mankind, and for the salvation of the entire world.[32]

54°. A suitable place may be found for the vernacular in Masses which are celebrated with the people, especially in the reading and "the common prayer", and also, as local conditions may warrant, in those parts which pertain to the people, according to the rules laid down in Article 36 of this Constitution.

Nevertheless steps should be taken so that the faithful may also be able to say or sing together in Latin those parts of the Ordinary of the Mass which pertain to them.

Whenever a more extended use of the vernacular in the Mass seems desirable the regulation laid down in Article 40 of this Constitution is to be observed.

55°. That more perfect form of participation in the Mass

---

[32] Cf. 1 Tim. 2:1-2.

whereby the faithful, after the priest's communion, receive the Lord's Body from the same sacrifice, is warmly recommended.

The dogmatic principles which were laid down by the Council of Trent remaining intact,[33] communion under both kinds may be granted when the bishops think fit, not only to clerics and religious but also to the laity, in cases to be determined by the Apostolic See. For example,

To the newly ordained in the Mass of their ordination;
To the newly professed in the Mass of their religious profession;
To the newly baptised in the Mass which follows their baptism.

56°. The two parts which in a sense go to make up the Mass, viz. the liturgy of the word and the eucharistic liturgy, are so closely connected with each other that they form but one single act of worship. Accordingly the sacred Synod strongly urges pastors of souls that, when instructing the faithful, they insistently teach them to take their part in the entire Mass, especially on Sundays and holydays of obligation.

CHAPTER III

THE OTHER SACRAMENTS AND THE SACRAMENTALS

59°. The purpose of the sacraments is to sanctify men, to build up the body of Christ, and, finally, to give worship to God. Because they are signs they also instruct. They not only presuppose faith, but by words and objects they also strengthen and express it. That is why they are called "sacraments of faith". They do, indeed, confer grace, but, in addition, the very act of celebrating them most effectively disposes the faithful to receive this grace in a fruitful manner, to worship God duly, and to practise charity.

It is, therefore, of the greatest importance that the faithful should easily understand the sacramental signs, and should frequent with the greatest eagerness those sacraments which were instituted to nourish the Christian life.

60°. Holy Mother Church has, moreover, instituted sacra-

[33] Council of Trent, Session 21: "On Communion under both Species", c. 1-3.

mentals. These are sacred signs which bear a resemblance to the sacraments. They signify effects, particularly of a spiritual nature, which are obtained through the Church's intercession. By them men are disposed to receive the chief effect of the sacraments, and various occasions in life are rendered holy.

61°. Thus, for well-disposed members of the faithful the liturgy of the sacraments and sacramentals sanctifies almost every event of their lives with the divine grace which flows from the paschal mystery of the Passion, Death and Resurrection of Christ. From this source all sacraments and sacramentals draw their power. There is scarcely any proper use of material things which cannot thus be directed towards the sanctification of men and the praise of God.

62°. With the passage of time, however, there have crept into the rites of the sacraments and sacramentals certain features which have rendered their nature and purpose far from clear to the people of today. Hence some changes are necessary to adapt them to present-day needs. For that reason the sacred Council decrees as follows concerning their revision:

63°. Because the use of the vernacular in the administration of the sacraments and sacramentals can often be of very great help to the people this use is to be extended according to the following norms:

(*a*) In the administration of the sacraments and sacramentals the vernacular may be used according to the norm of Article 36.

106°. By a tradition handed down from the apostles, which took its origin from the very day of Christ's resurrection, the Church celebrates the paschal mystery every eighth day, which day is appropriately called the Lord's Day or Sunday. For on this day Christ's faithful should come together into one place so that hearing the word of God and taking part in the Eucharist, they may call to mind the passion, resurrection and glory of the Lord Jesus, and may give thanks to God who "has begotten them again, through the resurrection of Christ from the dead, unto a living hope" (I Peter 1:3). The Lord's Day is the original feastday, and it should be proposed to the faithful and taught to them so that it may become in fact a day of joy and of freedom from work. Other celebrations, unless they be truly of the greatest importance, shall not have precedence over Sunday, which is the foundation and kernel of the whole liturgical year.

APPENDIX II

Instruction by the Sacred Congregation of Rites on the

PROPER IMPLEMENTING OF THE LITURGY CONSTITUTION[1]

PREFACE

NATURE OF THIS INSTRUCTION

1. It is only fitting that the Constitution on Sacred Liturgy should be amongst the first fruits of the Second Ecumenical Council of the Vatican, since it regulates the Church's noblest activities. It will yield fruit more abundantly, the more profoundly pastors and the faithful are truly imbued with its spirit and the more willingly they implement it.

2. The *Consilium* for the implementation of the Constitution on Sacred Liturgy—which Pope Paul VI established by the *Motu Proprio, Sacram Liturgiam* (25th January, 1964)—has energetically set about the task confided to it: the faithful execution of the prescriptions of the Constitution and of the *Motu Proprio,* their interpretation and implementation.

3. It is of the greatest importance that, from the very beginning, these documents should be rightly implemented everywhere and that all possible doubts as to their interpretation should be eliminated. It is for this reason that the *Consilium,* on the instructions of the Holy Father, has prepared the present Instruction. It defines more clearly the competence of episcopal conferences in liturgical matters, it makes more specific what was expressed in general terms in both documents, it permits, or decrees, certain changes which can be introduced prior to the revision of the liturgical books.

---

[1] The following translation was made by Father Austin Flannery, O.P., from the Latin text which was published in the *Osservatore Romano,* 18 October, 1964. The headings were in the original, the footnotes were added by the translator.

PRINCIPLES TO BE BORNE IN MIND

4. The practical directives which now follow have for their object to make the liturgy correspond more perfectly with the mind of the Council—to promote, that is to say, the active participation of the faithful. Further, the general reform of the liturgy will be better received by the faithful if it is accomplished gradually, and if it is proposed and explained to them properly by their pastors.

5. First of all, however, it is essential that everybody be persuaded that the scope of the Constitution on the Sacred Liturgy is not limited merely to the changing of liturgical rites and texts. Rather is it its aim to foster the formation of the faithful and that pastoral activity of which the liturgy is the summit and source (see Const., Art. 10). The changes in the liturgy which have already been introduced, or which will be introduced later, have this same end in view.

6. Pastoral activity which is centred on the liturgy aims to make the Paschal Mystery be expressed in men's lives.[2] It was in the Paschal Mystery that the Son of God incarnate, having been obedient unto the death of the cross, was raised so high by his resurrection and ascension that he was able to share his own divine life with the world, in such wise that men who had been dead to sin and were now made like to Christ "may not now live to themselves, but unto him who died for them, and rose again" (2 Cor. 5:15).

This is accomplished by faith and by the sacraments of faith—especially, that is to say, by baptism (see Const., Art. 6), by the sacred mystery of the Eucharist, the pivot of all the other sacraments and sacramentals (see Const., Art. 47), and also by the cycle of celebrations in which, throughout the Church's year, the paschal mystery of Christ is unfolded (see Const., Art. 102-107).

7. Consequently, even though the liturgy is not the whole of the Church's activity (see Const., Art. 9), great care must be taken that pastoral work be properly linked with it (*ut opera pastoralia cum sacra liturgia debite connectantur*). At the same time, the

[2] The Latin of this sentence is: *Vis autem huius actionis pastoralis circa Liturgiam ordinandae in eo posita est ut Mysterium paschale vivendo exprimatur*. The Italian translation published in the *Osservatore Romano* reads as follows: *Lo sforzo di questa azione pastorale incentrata nella liturgia deve tendere a far vivere il mistero pasquale.*

liturgical apostolate must not be exercised separately and, as it were, in a vacuum. It should be closely linked with other pastoral activities.

It is especially necessary that there be close links between liturgy, catechesis, religious instruction and preaching.

8. Bishops and their helpers in the priesthood, therefore, should set great store by their whole liturgy-centred apostolate. Thus the faithful too, by perfect participation in the liturgy will receive the divine life abundantly and, having become Christ's leaven and the salt of the earth, they will announce and transmit it to others.

CHAPTER I

CERTAIN GENERAL NORMS

HOW THESE NORMS WILL APPLY

9. The practical norms contained in the Constitution and in this Instruction as well as the changes which, even prior to the reform of the liturgical books, are by this same Instruction permitted or decreed, all apply solely to the Roman rite. However, they may be adopted by the other Latin rites, due allowance being made for the demands of the law.

10. Whatever measures this Instruction submits to the jurisdiction of the competent territorial ecclesiastical authority, it is this same authority, alone, which can and must put them into effect, by legitimate decrees.

In every case, the time and circumstances in which decrees become binding must be indicated. A sufficient interval of time should be allowed for notification of the faithful and for instructing them in the observance of the decrees.

LITURGICAL FORMATION OF THE CLERGY (Const., Art. 15, 16, 18)

11. With regard to the liturgical formation of the clergy:

(*a*) Theological faculties are to have a chair of liturgy, so that all students may be properly instructed in the liturgy; local ordinaries and major religious superiors should see to the provision, as soon as possible, of properly trained professors of liturgy in seminaries and in studentates for religious;

(*b*) Professors who are given charge of courses in sacred liturgy must be trained, as soon as possible, in accordance with Article 15 of the Constitution.

(*c*) Where possible, institutes of pastoral liturgy must be set up for further training of the clergy, especially of those who are already engaged in the apostolate.

12. Liturgy courses must be of appropriate duration, to be decided by the responsible authority, and must follow a proper method, in accordance with Article 15 of the Constitution.

13. Liturgical ceremonies should be celebrated with the utmost perfection. For this reason:

(*a*) The rubrics are to be observed carefully and the ceremonies to be performed with dignity, under the watchful scrutiny of the ecclesiastical superiors. They should be practised beforehand.

(*b*) Each cleric should frequently exercise the liturgical activities proper to his order; the activities, that is to say, of deacon, subdeacon, acolyte, reader and, further, commentator and chanter.

(*c*) Churches and oratories, church furnishings and vestments should be examples of genuine, modern Christian art.

LITURGICAL FORMATION OF THE SPIRITUAL LIFE OF THE CLERGY (Const., Art 17)

14. In seminaries and in studentates for religious the Constitution on Sacred Liturgy must be fully implemented, in accordance with the directives of the Holy See, and through the combined efforts of superiors and teachers; this to the end that the clerical students be taught to take part fully in the liturgical ceremonies and to draw from them nourishment both for their own spiritual lives and for communication to others later. They should be properly initiated into the liturgy, by the following means: by recommending to them, and by stocking their libraries with, a sufficient quantity of books which treat of the liturgy under its theological and spiritual aspects especially; by means of meditations and sermons drawn primarily from sacred scripture and from the liturgy (see Const., Art. 35, par. 2); by the communal

practice of all the traditional customs of the Christian life, in conformity with the liturgical seasons.

15. The daily celebration of the Eucharist, which is the centre of the spiritual life, should take the form best adapted to the condition of the participants (see Const., Art. 19).

On Sundays and on the greater feasts there should be Mass *in cantu* and all those who are at home should take part. There should be a homily and, as far as possible, those who are not priests should receive Holy Communion. Priests who are not needed for individual Masses for the faithful may concelebrate, especially on the more solemn feasts, after the new rite will have been published.

It is desirable (*expedit*) that seminarians should take part in the Eucharistic celebration with the bishop in the cathedral, at least on the great feasts (see Const., Art. 41).

16. It is very desirable that clerical students who are not yet bound to the divine office should recite or sing Lauds in common daily as morning prayer and Vespers as evening prayer, or Compline at the end of the day. As far as possible, the professors themselves should take part in this common exercise. Further, clerics who are in sacred orders should be given sufficient time for the recitation of the divine office through the day.

It is very desirable that, when possible, seminarians should sing Vespers in the cathedral, at least on the great feasts.

17. Pious practices which owe their origin to the customs or the laws of a locality or institute should be accorded due reverence. Care should be taken, however, especially if they are performed in common, that they be in keeping with the liturgy, in accordance with Article 13 of the Constitution, and that they take account of the liturgical seasons.

THE LITURGICAL FORMATION OF RELIGIOUS

18. What has been said in the foregoing articles about the spiritual formation of the clergy must be applied to members of the "states of perfection," both men and women.

LITURGICAL FORMATION OF THE FAITHFUL (Const., Art. 19)

19. Pastors of souls are to make it their business (*annitantur*) to implement, with care and patience, the precepts of the Constitution on the instruction of the faithful in the liturgy, and on their active participation in it, internally and externally, " taking

into account their age and condition, their way of life and standard of religious culture" (Const., Art. 19). They should take special care that members of religious associations for layfolk be instructed in the liturgy and take an active part in it. It is the role of such associations to share more intimately in the life of the Church and to assist pastors in organising the liturgical life of the parish (see Const., Art. 42).

THE COMPETENT AUTHORITY IN LITURGICAL MATTERS (Const., Art. 22)

20. It belongs to the Church's authority to regulate the sacred liturgy. Nobody, therefore, is allowed to proceed on his own initiative in this domain, for this would be to the detriment of the liturgy itself, more often than not, and of the reform which the competent authority has to carry out.

21. It is for the Holy See to reform and to approve liturgical books for general use, to regulate the sacred liturgy for the universal Church, to approve or confirm the "Acts" and deliberations of the territorial authorities and to receive the proposals or petitions of these same territorial authorities.

22. It is for the bishop to regulate the liturgy in his own diocese, in accordance with the norms and the spirit of the Constitution on Sacred Liturgy, the decrees of the Holy See and of the competent territorial authority.

DIVISION OF LITURGICAL FUNCTIONS TO BE OBSERVED (Const., Art. 28)

32. If the parts which belong to the choir and the people are chanted or recited by them, they must not be said privately by the celebrant.

33. Similarly, the celebrant must not say privately the readings which are read or sung by the competent minister or the altar-server.

NOT RESPECTING PERSONS (Const., Art. 32)

34. Bishops—or, if it seems opportune, regional or national episcopal conferences—are to see to the implementation, in their territories, of the prescription of the holy Council which forbids the according of special honours, either in ceremonies or by external display, to private persons or to social classes.

35. For the rest, in liturgical ceremonies, and especially in the celebration of Mass and in the administration of the sacraments and of the sacramentals, pastors should, with prudence and charity, see to it that the equality of all the faithful is expressed, even externally, and that any appearance of money-making is avoided (*ut . . . omnis species quaestus vitetur*).

THE SIMPLIFICATION OF CERTAIN RITES (Const., Art. 34)

36. In order that liturgical ceremonies may have that noble simplicity which is in keeping with the mind of our age:

(*a*) obeisances (*inclinationes*) by celebrants and ministers to the choir will be made only at the beginning and the end of sacred ceremonies;

(*b*) incensation of the clergy, apart from those who are bishops, is to be made collectively, by a triple incensation to each part of the choir;

(*c*) only the altar at which the liturgical ceremony takes place is to be incensed;

(*d*) the kissing of hands and of objects given or received is to be omitted.

CHAPTER II

THE EUCHARISTIC MYSTERY

THE ORDER OF THE MASS (Const., Art. 50)

48. Until the entire Order of the Mass will have been reformed, the following directives are to be observed:

(*a*) The portions of the Proper which are sung or recited by the choir or by the people are not to be said privately by the celebrant.

(*b*) The portions of the Ordinary may be sung or recited with the choir or people by the celebrant.

(*c*) In the prayers said at the foot of the altar at the beginning of Mass, Psalm 42 is to be omitted. All the prayers at the foot of the altar are to be omitted whenever another liturgical function immediately precedes the celebration of Mass.

(*d*) In a solemn Mass, the paten is not held by the subdeacon, but is left on the altar.

(*e*) The Secret, or "prayer over the offerings", is to be chanted at Masses *in cantu* and in other Masses is to be said aloud.

(*f*) The doxology at the end of the Canon of the Mass, from the words *Per ipsum* to *Per omnia saecula saeculum,* and the response *Amen,* inclusively, are to be chanted or said aloud. During the whole of the doxology the celebrant is to hold the chalice and the host slightly elevated, he is to omit the signs of the cross and, at the end, he is to genuflect only after the people have answered *Amen.*

(*g*) The "Our Father" can be said in the vernacular by the people and celebrant at said Masses; at Masses *in cantu,* however, celebrant and people may sing it together in Latin or, if the territorial ecclesiastical authority so decree, in the vernacular, using a melody approved by the same authority.

(*h*) The embolism which follows the Our Father, is to be chanted or said aloud.

(*i*) The formula *Corpus Christi* is to be used in the distribution of Holy Communion. As he says the words, the celebrant is to hold the host, slightly elevated, over the ciborium, showing it to the communicant, who is to reply, *Amen.* The celebrant then gives him Holy Communion, omitting the sign of the cross with the host.

(*j*) The last gospel is to be omitted; the Leonine prayers are suppressed.

(*k*) It is permissible to celebrate Mass *in cantu,* with a deacon only.

(*l*) When necessary, bishops may celebrate Mass *in cantu* after the manner of priests.

THE READINGS AND THE INTERVENING CHANTS (Const., Art. 51)

49. In public Masses, the Lessons, the Epistle and the Gospel, are to be read or sung facing the people:

(*a*) at a solemn Mass, from an ambo or at the altar-rails;

(*b*) at a sung Mass and at a said Mass, if it is the celebrant who is reading or chanting them, he may do so from the altar, from the ambo, or from the altar-rails, whichever is the more suitable; if anybody else is reading or singing them, however, he must do so from the ambo or the altar-rails.

50. In non-solemn, public Masses, the Lessons and the Epistle, together with the intervening chants, can be read by a suitable reader or altar-server, the celebrant being seated and listening; the Gospel, however, can be read by a deacon or a priest, who is to say *Munda cor meum,* ask for a blessing and, at the end, offer the book of the Gospels to the celebrant to be kissed.

51. In Masses *in cantu,* if the vernacular is used for the Lessons, the Epistle and Gospel, they may read, the chanting of them being dispensed with.

52. When the Lessons, the Epistle, the intervening chants and the Gospel are being read or sung, the following procedure is to be observed:

(*a*) In a solemn Mass, the celebrant, seated, listens to the Lessons, the Epistle and the intervening chants. When the Epistle has been sung or read, the subdeacon goes to the celebrant and is blessed by him. Then the celebrant, seated, puts incense into the thurible and blesses it. While the *Alleluia* and verse is being sung—or towards the end of whatever other chants follow the Epistle—the celebrant rises and blesses the deacon; standing at the seat, he listens to the Gospel, kisses the Gospel-book and, after the homily, intones the Creed, if it is to be sung. After the Creed has been finished, he returns to the altar with his ministers, unless he has to direct the "prayer of the faithful".

(*b*) In sung Masses or said Masses in which the Lessons, the Epistle, the chants which follow the Epistle, and the Gospel, are chanted or read by a minister, as outlined in number 50, the celebrant should follow the directives given above.

(*c*) In sung Masses and said Masses in which he himself reads or chants the Gospel in an ambo or at the altar-rails, the celebrant goes over to the altar while the *Alleluia* and verse is being sung—or towards the end of whatever chants follow the Epistle—and, bowing in front of the lowest altar step, he says *Munda cor meum* and then goes to the ambo or the altar-rails to sing or read the Gospel.

(*d*) If, however, during a sung Mass or a said Mass the celebrant himself sings or reads all the readings in the ambo or at the altar-rails, he must read the intervening chants in the same place. He says *Munda cor meum*, however, facing the altar.

THE HOMILY (Const., Art. 52)

53. There must be a homily at every public Mass on Sundays and holydays of obligation. No exception is made for sung conventual Mass or for pontifical Mass. Apart from holydays, it is recommended that there be a homily on certain ferial days during Advent and Lent, and on other occasions when the faithful go to church in larger numbers.

54. The "homily from the sacred text" is to be understood to be either an explanation of certain aspects of the readings from Sacred Scripture, or of some other text from the Ordinary or the Proper of the day, taking into account, however, the mystery which is being celebrated and the peculiar needs of the congregation.

55. If a scheme for preaching is drawn up for certain times of the year, it should be closely and harmoniously linked with —at least—the principal seasons and feasts of the liturgical year (see Const., Art. 102-104). It should be linked, that is to say, with the mystery of the Redemption. The homily is part of the liturgy of the day.

THE PRAYER OF THE FAITHFUL (Const., Art. 53)

56. Where the "community prayer", or the "prayer of the faithful",[3] has already become customary, it should be said before the Offertory and after the *Oremus,* using the formulae existing in each region, for the time being. The celebrant is to direct the prayer from the celebrant's seat, or from the altar, the ambo or the altar-rails.

The intentions or invocations can be sung by a deacon, a chanter, or by some other suitable server. The celebrant, however, is to say the words of introduction and the concluding

[3] Father Reinhold gives a sample, composed by Father Balthasar Fischer, in his *Bringing the Mass to the People,* pp. 56-57. Another sample is contained in the Good Friday liturgy. See also *L'Eglise en Prière,* by G. Martimort, Paris 1962, pp. 358-360.

prayer, which, normally, will be the prayer "God our refuge and our strength" (see *Missale Romanum, Orationes diversae*, No. 20). An alternative prayer which answers better to a particular need may be substituted for it, however.

Where, however, the "community prayer", or "prayer of the faithful", is not customary, the competent territorial ecclesiastical authority can order it to be done, along the lines indicated above, using, for the time being, formulae approved by itself.

WHERE THE VERNACULAR MAY BE USED IN THE MASS (Const., Art. 54)

57. The competent territorial ecclesiastical authority, its "Acts" being subject to the approval or confirmation of the Holy See, can allow the vernacular in public Masses, whether *in cantu* or said, as follows:

(*a*) for the Lessons, the Epistle and Gospel, and in the "prayer of the faithful", especially;

(*b*) as local conditions suggest, in the chants of the Ordinary of the Mass—in the *Kyrie, Gloria, Credo, Sanctus-Benedictus* and *Agnus Dei*—in the Introit, Offertory and Communion antiphons, and in the chants between the readings;

(*c*) further, in the acclamations, the salutations and the dialogue formulae, in the formulae: *Ecce Agnus Dei, Domine non sum dignus* and *Corpus Christi* in the communion of the faithful, and in the Lord's Prayer, the introductory admonition to it, and its embolism.

Missals for liturgical use, however, must have the Latin text as well as the vernacular text.

58. Only the Holy See can grant permission for the vernacular in the other parts of the Mass which are said by the celebrant alone.

59. Pastors of souls should take care that the faithful, and especially those who are members of pious associations of layfolk, are also able to recite or sing in Latin—at any rate, in the simpler melodies—the portions of the Ordinary of the Mass which pertain to them.

REPEATING HOLY COMMUNION ON THE SAME DAY (Const., Art. 55)

60. The faithful who have received Holy Communion during the Mass of the Easter Vigil, or during the Mass of the night of the Lord's Nativity, may receive Holy Communion again at the second Paschal Mass and at one of the Masses of Christmas Day.

CHAPTER V

ON BUILDING CHURCHES AND ALTARS FOR ACTIVE PARTICIPATION

THE PLANNING OF CHURCHES

90. In erecting new churches, or in reconstructing or adapting existing churches, care should be taken that they be suitable for the performance of sacred actions, as befits their true nature, and for the promotion of the active participation of the faithful (see Const., Art. 124).

THE HIGH ALTAR

91. It is important that between the high altar and the wall of the church there be sufficient space to enable one to go right around the altar easily, and so that Mass facing the people can be celebrated on it. It should be so placed in the sacred building that, automatically, it becomes the true focus of attention for the entire congregation of the faithful.

In the selection of materials for building and ornamenting the altar, the prescriptions of the law are to be observed.

The sanctuary should be large enough to allow for the proper performance of the sacred ceremonies.

THE SEAT FOR THE CELEBRANT AND MINISTERS

92. A seat for the celebrant and ministers, which should harmonise with the structure of the church, should be so placed that it will be clearly visible by the faithful, and that the celebrant himself will be clearly seen to be presiding over the assembly.

At the same time, if the seat is placed behind the altar, it should not look like a throne, for this is reserved for the bishop alone.

SIDE ALTARS

93. Side altars should be few in number. In fact, if the building allows this, it is very fitting (*valde congruit*) to put them in chapels somewhat removed from the main part of the church.

ALTAR FURNISHINGS

94. The crucifix and the candles which are needed for the different liturgical actions can, if the local ordinary so judges, be put near the altar.

THE RESERVATION OF THE EUCHARIST

95. The Blessed Sacrament is to be reserved in a solid, inviolable tabernacle, which should be placed in the middle of the high altar, or on a side altar which really stands out (*altaris minoris, sed vere praecellentis*). It may also, in accordance with the legitimate custom and in individual instances approved by the local ordinary, be placed in some other place in the church, provided it is really dignified and properly ornamented.

It is permissible to say Mass facing the people even when there is a tabernacle on the altar; it must, of course, be small, though suitable for its purpose.

THE AMBO

96. It is fitting to have an ambo, or ambos, for the sacred readings. They should be so placed that the ministers using them can be clearly seen and heard by the people.

THE CHOIR AND THE ORGAN

97. The choir and the organ should be so placed as to make it clear that the singers and the organist form part of the congregation, and to enable them to carry out their liturgical functions properly.

THE SPACE FOR THE FAITHFUL

98. The space for the faithful is to be planned with special care, so as to enable them to take part properly in the sacred actions, with eyes and heart. Normally, it is good to provide pews or seats, for their use. The custom of reserving seats for private individuals, however, is to be reprobated, in accordance with Article 32 of the Constitution.

Care should be taken that the faithful are not only able to see the celebrant and other ministers, but that, with the help of modern amplifying systems, they are able to hear them easily also.

His Eminence, Giacomo Cardinal Lercaro, transmitted this Instruction to His Holiness, Pope Paul VI. It has been prepared by the "Consilium" for the Implementation of the Constitution on Sacred Liturgy, by command of His Holiness.

His Holiness examined the Instruction with all necessary care, being assisted in this both by the "Consilium" and by the Sacred Congregation of Rites. On 26th September, in an audience granted to His Eminence Arcadio Maria Cardinal Larraona, the Prefect of the Sacred Congregation of Rites, he granted it his special approval, as a whole and in its parts, he confirmed it with his own authority, and ordered it to be published, and to be carefully observed by all concerned, as from 7th March, 1965, the First Sunday of Lent.

Given at Rome, 26th September, 1964.

GIACOMO CARDINAL LERCARO
Archbishop of Bologna,
President of the "Consilium" for the Implementation
of the Constitution on Sacred Liturgy

ARCADIO M. CARDINAL LARRAONA
Prefect S.C.R.

✠ ENRICO DANTE
Archbishop tit. Carpathia
Secretary, S.C.R.